Margaret-Anne Colgan • Monique Mainella • Michael
In collaboration with
Gwenn Gauthier • Leena M. Sandblom

English as a Second Language   Secondary Cycle Two, Year One

PRIME TIME

Student Book

LES ÉDITIONS
CEC
QUEBECOR MEDIA

8101, boul. Métropolitain Est, Anjou (Québec) Canada H1J 1J9
Téléphone : 514-351-6010 • Télécopieur : 514-351-3534

Editorial Managers
Carolyn Faust
Julie Hough

Production Manager
Danielle Latendresse

Project Editors
Michèle Devlin
Kathryn Rhoades

Copy Editors
Roberto Blizzard
Brian Parsons

Rights Research
Shona French
Line Madore

Photo Research
Line Madore
Monique Rosevear

Cover and page layout
Dessine-moi un mouton

Page design
2NSB et Dessin-moi un mouton

Illustrations
Claude Bordeleau, Yves Boudreau, Jean-Paul Eid, Élisabeth Eudes-Pascal

Les Éditions CEC inc. remercient le gouvernement du Québec de l'aide financière accordée à l'édition de cet ouvrage par l'entremise du Programme de crédit d'impôt pour l'édition de livres, administré par la SODEC.

Prime Time, Student Book, Secondary Cycle Two, Year One
© 2007, Les Éditions CEC inc.
8101, boul. Métropolitain Est
Anjou (Québec) H1J 1J9

Dépôt légal : 2007
Bibliothèque et Archives nationales du Québec
Bibliothèque et Archives du Canada

ISBN : 978-2-7617-2478-4

Imprimé au Canada
1 2 3 4 5 11 10 09 08 07

Acknowledgements

The authors wish to thank all the team at Les Éditions CEC for their incredible hard work and dedication. Deepest thanks to Julie Hough who started us on a wonderful path of discovery and to Carolyn Faust who continued the journey with us, keeping us sane and grounded, all with a smile and a pat on the back. Special thanks to Gwenn Gauthier and Leena Sandblom.

Personal thanks go to the following people:

To Dominic, without whom I would not be who or where I am today. To Jean-Pierre, Anthony and Liam, you guys are simply the best – MAC

To my family, friends and my husband Vince for their loving and never-ending support, thank you – MM

To Anna Guardia, for her love and understanding – MON

And finally, we wish to thank the many teachers who participated in our various consultations. Their insights helped ensure that *Prime Time* really works.

Table of Contents

It's Prime Time

> These pages will explain what your Student Book has in store for you.

> There are twelve units, four of them projects, all about interesting topics related to you and your life.

- The first two pages of each unit introduce the theme of the unit.
  - *Ask Yourself* questions help focus your attention on the issues you will explore in the unit.

- A variety of tasks help you discover more about the theme and learn new language.
  - *Word Wise* boxes suggest language that is useful for oral interaction.
  - *Glossary* boxes give definitions of unfamiliar words and expressions. These appear in bold on the page.
  - *FYI (For Your Information)* boxes provide cultural information linked to the theme.

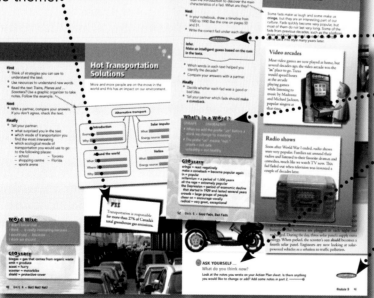

- *Strategy* boxes suggest ways to improve your communication and comprehension skills.

- *What's in a Word?* boxes ask you to look more closely at the language you are using.

- *Ask yourself ... What do you think now?* encourages you to reflect on the issues and adjust your opinion.

- The *Vocabulary* ovals remind you to add words to your vocabulary log.

- **Language Works** pages focus on conversation and co-operative activities.

  - Language models suggest expressions that will help you begin and maintain conversations throughout the activities.

  - Recordings let you listen to authentic conversations linked to the theme of the unit.

  - Interesting activities allow you to express your opinion, explain your point of view and discuss solutions to relevant problems with classmates.

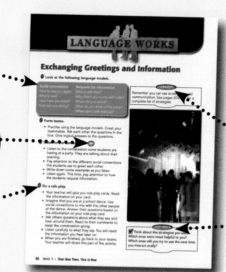

- *Strategy* boxes used here remind you to use appropriate strategies to communicate.

- *Self-check* boxes help you reflect on the strategies you used.

- **Grammar Works** pages allow you to review and practise grammar structures featured in the texts and tasks of the unit.

  - The introductory activities let you demonstrate what you already know.

  - Charts explain the form and uses of the targeted grammar structures.

  - Practice activities let you use the grammar in context.

  - *Grammar Works* boxes focus your attention on specific grammar points in the texts.

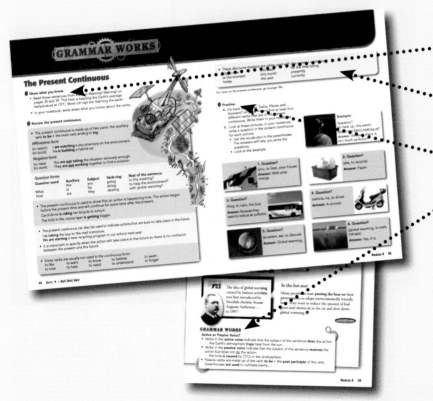

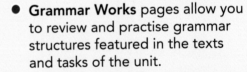

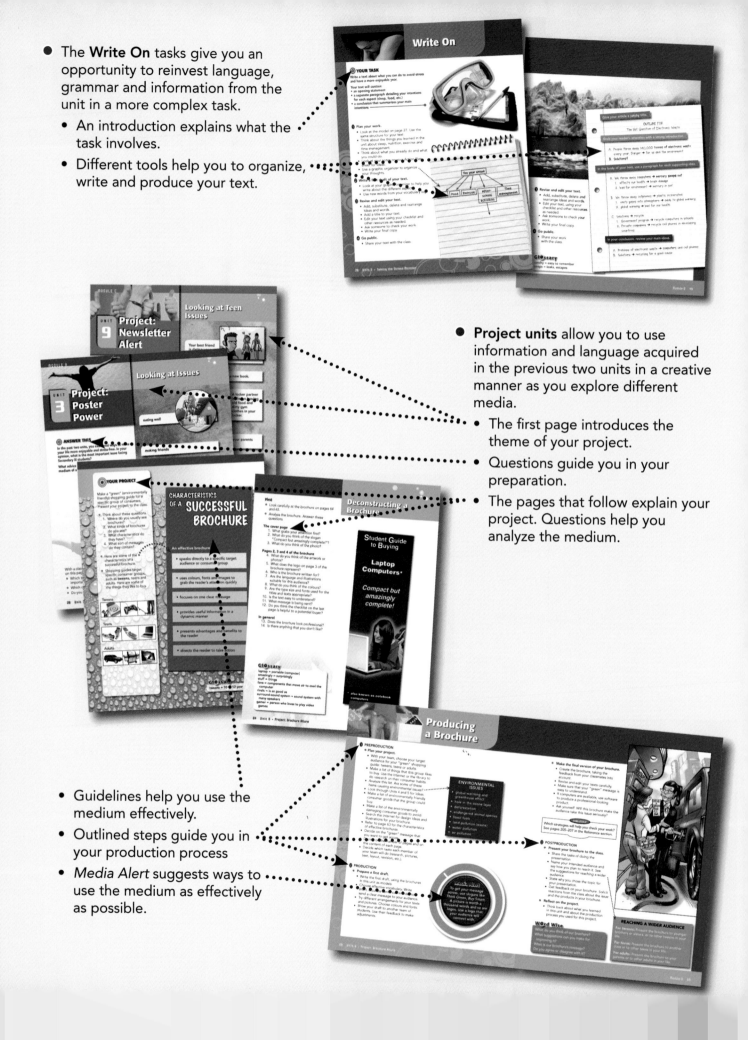

- The **Write On** tasks give you an opportunity to reinvest language, grammar and information from the unit in a more complex task.
  - An introduction explains what the task involves.
  - Different tools help you to organize, write and produce your text.

- **Project units** allow you to use information and language acquired in the previous two units in a creative manner as you explore different media.
  - The first page introduces the theme of your project.
  - Questions guide you in your preparation.
  - The pages that follow explain your project. Questions help you analyze the medium.

- Guidelines help you use the medium effectively.
- Outlined steps guide you in your production process
- *Media Alert* suggests ways to use the medium as effectively as possible.

- An **Anthology** section contains a variety of texts that you can read for pleasure and improve your reading skills.

- A **Vocabulary** section organized by module provides:
  - Words and expressions in alphabetical order.
  - Definitions in context.

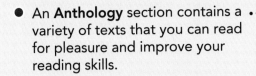

- A **Reference** section that contains:
  - A review of all grammar structures seen in the units.
  - A *Spell Well* box that focuses on spelling rules for the grammar point.
  - A summary of functional language expressions.
  - A complete list of strategies.
  - An overview of the response, writing and production processes.

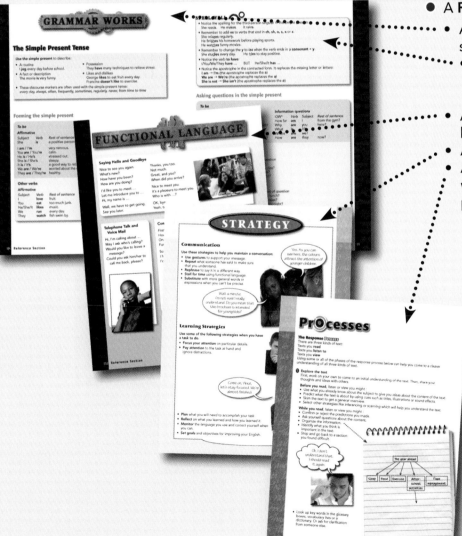

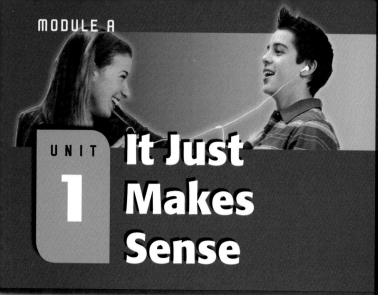

UNIT 1 It Just Makes Sense

◎ ASK YOURSELF ...

Do you think that your senses have anything to do with your health and well-being? Which of your senses is most important to you? Write down your thoughts about these questions on your Action Plan sheet. ────────○

- Try this quiz to see how **sense-savvy** you are. You have 10 minutes to do it.

- Give yourself one point per correct answer.

Glossary

makes sense = is logical
sense-savvy = well informed about senses
quickly = rapidly
sensible = reasonable, realistic

Test Your Senses

What do you know about your senses?

1. What is the colour of the letters in each word? Write down your answers **quickly**.

a) **RED**　　　b) **BROWN**

c) **GREEN**　　d) **BLUE**

e) **YELLOW**　　f) **BLACK**

2. Which of these can you see, touch, smell <u>and</u> taste?
   a) a glass of water
   b) a glass of orange juice
   c) an empty glass

How sense-savvy are you?

- 8 points: Sensational! You know your senses.

- 6 or 7 points: Sensitive! That's what you are.

- 4 or 5 points: You're a **sensible** person. You will make sense of all your senses in no time.

- Less than 4 points: Maybe your sensory perceptions are off today.

3. How many T's are there in this sentence? Count them quickly and only once.

I wanted to go to the movie at the mall today but Tina couldn't come.

6. Which of these sentences has an error in it?

a) I LOVE THE SMELL OF HOT POPCORN AT THE MOVIES.

b) I LOVE TO LOOK AT THE THE STARS IN A SUMMER SKY.

c) I LOVE THE TASTE OF APPLE PIE AND ICE CREAM.

4. Place these sounds in order from the loudest sound to the quietest.
a) Alarm clock
b) Rock concert
c) Helicopter
d) Car
e) Screaming child

7. How many taste buds do babies have?
a) 2,000
b) 5,000
c) 10,000

5. What is the least sensitive part of your body?
a) Your neck
b) Your arms
c) The middle of your back

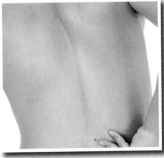

8. Look at the two red circles. Are they the same size?
a) Yes
b) No

What's in a Word?

• Why are the following words easy to understand?
SENSATIONAL   SENSITIVE   SENSES   SENSORY

First

- Work alone on TEXT 1, *The Nose Knows*.
- Look at the title, subtitle and illustration.
- Scan the text for new words. Use the glossary below and the vocabulary section on page 170 to understand them.
- Read the text and complete the reading log.

STRATEGY

Focus your attention.
Look at your reading log. What information should you focus on as you read?

Next

- With a partner, compare your reading log answers. If you don't agree, check the text.

And now

- Find out what other senses do.
- Form teams of three. Discuss how you want to read the other texts:
  - You can work together on all three texts.
  - You can each read one text and tell each other what you learned.
  - You can read the three texts on your own and then compare your answers.
- Use the reading logs to help you understand and think about the texts.

Glossary

mood = state of mind, feeling
trigger = set off a reaction
awaken = bring back, evoke
stress-busting = that reduce stress
relieve = reduce, stop
warm and fuzzy = happy and relaxed

Making Sense of Your Senses

Your senses not only help you perceive the world around you, they also affect your **mood**, mind and body. Read on to see how.

TEXT 1   The Nose Knows

The smell of freshly baked cookies, burning firewood, buttery popcorn—do these odours remind you of anything? They should. Odours **trigger** memories and emotions. The olfactory
5 receptors in your nose are connected to your limbic system, the part of your brain responsible for emotions, motivation and memory. Some odours can **awaken** very pleasant memories. Scents can have a dramatic
10 effect on your mood. ●

Stress-busting smells

Any smell that a person likes should have a positive effect. Certain smells can affect people in a very specific way. For example, vanilla has a
15 relaxing effect. The smell of lemons helps make you more alert for studying. Smelling lavender can reduce stress. The smell of green apples can help **relieve** headache pain, and the scent of oranges can help fight depression. In fact, just
20 thinking about pleasant odours may make you feel better. So what smell makes you feel **warm and fuzzy** inside? Think of that smell the next time you find yourself in a stressful situation. ●

TEXT 2 **Touchy-Feely**

Do you know what the biggest human organ is? Believe it or not, it's your skin. Your skin is responsible for receiving and sending messages to your brain through your sense of touch.
5 What you touch and how your skin is touched can affect your mood and health. ●

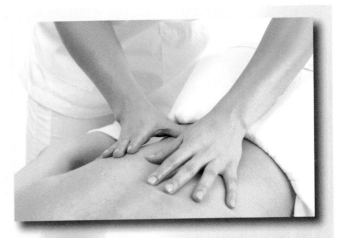

Everyone's into it
Getting a massage is the most common form of stress relief. It relaxes your muscles and
10 affects your mood in a positive way. It can even help reduce depression. That's because massages increase blood circulation and reduce stress hormones.

The benefits of massages are taken very
15 seriously in sports. Athletes get their muscles massaged before and after training to prevent **injury**. They also get massages before a competition to relieve stress and **improve** performance.

20 Massages help travellers, too. To relieve the stress of travelling, some airports now offer 15-minute massages while you wait to board the plane. Getting a quick massage anytime is very easy: just use your own hands to
25 massage your neck and shoulders. ●

Physical contact through your skin can help you relax.

Give a dog a hug
Did you know that **petting** animals is good for you? Petting a dog or cat can actually reduce your blood pressure. Dogs are often used in
30 nursing homes to help **ease** pain and stress in people during physical rehabilitation. So the next time you feel anxious, do something about it. Try a massage, or pet a cat or dog and relax, relax, relax! ●

Glossary
touchy-feely = very sensitive and affectionate
injury = damage to the body
improve = ameliorate, help to make better
petting = stroking or smoothing the coat of
    an animal to give affection
ease = reduce

TEXT 3 I Hear You Loud and Clear

Love listening to your favorite song? The kind of music you listen to can really have a powerful impact when you feel sick, sad or **stressed out**. When you are **tense**, try listening to classical
5 music or other slow music. The slower beat has a relaxing effect on the body and mind. If you want to feel energized, you need a faster beat that will affect your mood in a positive way. ●

Music is not the only sound that can make you
10 feel good. Going for a nature walk and listening to the birds singing or listening to a recording of the ocean can help you relax before an important exam or presentation. ●

Just laugh it off

15 Better still, the sound of your own laughter will make you feel better. It will even improve your health. Laughing reduces the stress hormones in your body. It also stimulates your immune system so you are better able to **fight off**
20 infections and diseases.

So **listen up**! Music, the sounds of nature and laughter are all around you, just
25 ready to make you feel good. ●

TEXT 4 The World Through Your Eyes

Our eyes are our windows on the world. What we look at could have an impact on our mood and health. Scientists have long studied the effects of colours on our state of mind and
5 well-being. Some colours have specific effects. For example, looking at the colours pink, green and blue often has a relaxing effect on the body and mind. Yellow is a memory trigger. The colour orange reduces fatigue and stimulates
10 the appetite, so restaurants and cafeterias are often painted orange. The next time you walk into a room, **check out** the colour of the walls and see how it makes you feel. ●

15 ### Watching the fish go by

But it's not just colour that affects the body and mind. Looking at fish swim in an aquarium also has health benefits. It lowers blood pressure and anxiety, and has a calming effect. Dentists' offices
20 often have aquariums to help patients relax before they sit in the chair. So the next time you feel uneasy, stop by the pet shop and watch the fish swim around—it just might help. ●

Your mind reacts to the images your eyes send.

VOCABULARY

Glossary

stressed out = tired, anxious because of stress
tense = not able to relax, under stress
laugh it off = not take something seriously
fight off = combat
listen up = pay attention
check out = pay attention to
FYI = for your information
lack of sight = not being able to see
blind = unable to see

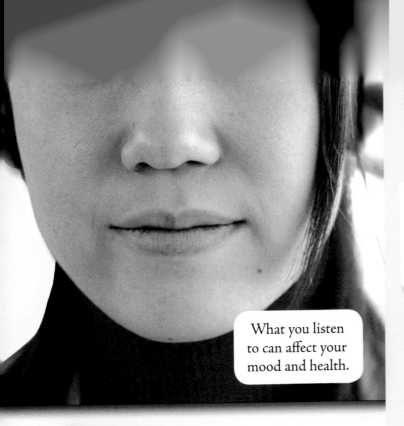

What you listen to can affect your mood and health.

FYI

Lack of sight doesn't stop true hockey fans. There are teams for **blind** and visually impaired players all across Canada. The game is played like regular hockey but with adjustments made to the equipment and rules. For example, some teams use a can or a metal puck filled with metal pieces so that it can be heard. Most teams play sighted teams with very few adjustments to their rules. They rely on sound, instinct and their knowledge of the game to take part in a typically Canadian sport.

◉ ASK YOURSELF …

What do you think now?

Look at the notes you wrote on your Action Plan sheet. Now, look over the senses chart you filled in. Have you changed your mind about anything? Do you have any new ideas? Write them down in part 2.

Finally

- Do a follow-up on your reading by completing a senses chart. Follow this example.

Text #	Benefits for …		
	mood	stress	health
1. The Nose Knows		Vanilla has a relaxing effect.	

- If you worked in teams, take turns telling your teammates the benefits described in each text. Enter the key information in the senses chart.
- If you worked alone, you can complete the senses chart on your own and then compare charts with a partner.

A closer look

- Go back to Text 3.
- Look at its structure.
  - Is there an opening question or statement near the beginning of the text?
  - Does the text give an explanation and some examples related to the question or statement?
  - Is there a strong final statement in the text?

GRAMMAR WORKS

–ING words
Remember that –ING words can have several functions:
- adjective: a **relaxing** effect
- noun: **Laughing** reduces stress.
- verb in a continuous tense: Jade **is listening** to music.

First

- Take this quiz to find out how much you know about your tongue.
- Are the statements true or false?
- Share your answers with a partner.

Then

- Discover some interesting facts about your tongue.
- Which facts surprised you?

Finally

- Read about cranium cramp. Has this ever happened to you?
- Try a tongue twister.

Your tongue is very important. Without it, you wouldn't be able to eat, taste, sing or even speak.

True or False?

1. Boys have **fewer** taste buds than girls.
2. Taste is weaker than the other four senses.
3. Your tongue rests while you sleep.
4. The strongest muscle in the body is the tongue.
5. Butterflies taste their food with their feet.
6. It is impossible to **lick** your elbow.
7. Every person has a unique tongue print.
8. A crocodile cannot **stick out** its tongue.

Licking a stamp adds 1/10 of a calorie to your diet.

People generally lose half their taste buds by the time they are 60 years old.

Taste and smell are interconnected. If you block your nose while eating, it is hard to identify taste.

Five taste sensations have been identified: sweet, bitter, savoury, salty and sour.

You will produce more than 23,000 litres of saliva in your lifetime.

Your tongue grows new taste buds every two weeks.

People have been piercing their tongues since prehistoric times.

Cranium Cramp!

It's a hot summer day and you reach for an ice-cold drink. You **take a big gulp** and then, ouch! Your brain hurts. You are suffering from sphenopalatine ganglioneuralgia, better known
5 as brain freeze, cranium cramp or ice cream headache.

When very cold drinks or foods touch the centre of your palate, the cold can trigger a nerve reaction that causes the blood vessels in
10 your brain to **swell**. Those swollen blood vessels give you a headache. The headache usually lasts only a minute but it is very intense and unpleasant.

To stop the pain, you can press your tongue to
15 the roof of your mouth or drink a glass of warm water. To avoid brain freeze, eat cold foods slowly and **sip** those ice-cold drinks. Let the food or drink warm up a bit in your mouth before you swallow. Finally, slow down and take
20 the time to enjoy your treat!

Now it's time to put your tongue to work. Pair up with a partner and see how many times you can say this tongue twister without making a mistake.

TONGUE IN A KNOT

Sally senses Sammy's stress
so Sally sings silly songs
and Sammy sings along.

Glossary

fewer = a smaller number of
lick = use your tongue to eat or wash
stick out = push out
take a big gulp = drink quickly
swell = become bigger or thicker
sip = drink a small amount of liquid

Modals

1 Show what you know.

- Find the modals in the following sentences.
  A. The scent of oranges can help fight depression and sadness.
  B. Just thinking about pleasant odours might help you feel better.
  C. The next time you feel anxious, you must do something about it.
  D. When you are tense, you should listen to slow music.

- Draw this chart in your notebook and complete it with modals from the sentences.

an obligation	a possibility	a suggestion	an ability

2 Review modals.

Certain auxiliaries, called modals, express ability, possibility or obligation. Modals are also used to make suggestions and give advice.
Notice that the modal **precedes** the main verb, and that the main verb is always in the **base form** (the infinitive without *to*).

Ability	Listening to music **can** improve your mood. Max **can't** relax before a presentation. Mary **is able to** relieve tension by petting her cat.
Possibility	I **might** take up yoga. Lucy **may** get a massage. They **may not** like the smell of green apples.
Obligation	You **must** try to relax. I **musn't** worry so much. He **has to** get plenty of sleep.
(No obligation)	You **don't have to** be perfect.
Suggestion	They **could** watch a funny movie. She **should** try aromatherapy.

Hi, Paul. I have a presentation tomorrow and I'm so stressed out. What should I do?

For more on modals, go to page 196.

3 Practise.

- Give some good advice to a friend who is feeling stressed out about an upcoming presentation.
- Use five different modals. Look at your senses chart for ideas.

LANGUAGE WORKS

Expressing Your Point of View

1 **Look at the following language models.**

Expressing feelings and preferences	Discourse markers	Stalling for time
I would prefer to ...	First of all, ...	I mean, ...
I feel ...	On the other hand, ...	You know, ...
I really need ...	However, ...	All right, ...

2 **Form teams.**

- Brainstorm for other language you already know for expressing feelings or preferences and for stalling for time.

3 **Listen to the conversation.** 🎧

- These students are discussing which sense is the most important of all.
- Pay attention to the language they use to express feelings and preferences and to stall for time.
- Write down a few examples as you listen.

4 **Defend your point of view.**
If you were told you had to give up all your senses except one, which sense would you keep?

- Get into teams of four.
- Write the following words on four slips of paper: TOUCH, SMELL, SIGHT and HEARING. Take turns and pick one of the senses. You are now responsible for defending that sense.
- Use information from the unit to help you justify why the sense you picked should be the one to stay. Think about the following questions to guide you in finding good arguments.
- How is life easier and better because of this sense?
- How would life be more difficult without it?

STRATEGY

Remember you can use strategies to aid communication. See pages 205–207 for a complete list of strategies.

Write On

◎ YOUR TASK

Write a text explaining how you can use each sense to reduce stress and improve your health. Say which sense is most important to you and why.

Your text will contain:
- an opening question or statement
- a separate paragraph for each sense
- a conclusion that states which sense is most important to you and why ───────○

1 **Plan your writing.**
- Look at the model on page 13. Use the same structure for your text.
- Use the texts on pages 4 to 6 as models.
- Think about the things you learned in this unit about smell, touch, hearing and sight.
- Look at your Action Plan notes and your senses chart for ideas.
- Use a chart to organize the information ⋯⋯⋯ for each sense.

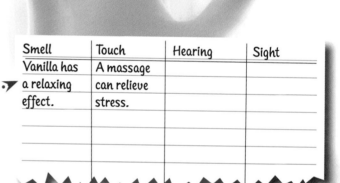

Smell	Touch	Hearing	Sight
Vanilla has a relaxing effect.	A massage can relieve stress.		

2 **Write a first draft of your text.**
- Look at your chart to help you write about every sense.
- Use new words from your vocabulary log.

3 **Revise and edit your text.**
- Add, substitute, delete and rearrange ideas and words.
- Edit your text using your checklist and other resources as needed.
- Ask someone to check your work.
- Write your final copy.

4 **Go public.**
- Share your text with the class.

A good opening question or statement

How can I use my senses to reduce stress? ...

Details on what you can do with each sense to lower stress

When I feel stressed, I can listen to ...

I don't have a dog, but I can ...

I really like the smell of ...

My favourite colour is ...

A strong conclusion

All these senses are important to me, but the most important ...

Glossary
pick-me-up = good experience that makes you happier

UNIT 2 Taming the Stress Monster

ASK YOURSELF ...

Here you are, in your middle year in secondary school. Are you busier than ever? What can you do to avoid stress and have a more enjoyable year? Write down your ideas and opinions on your Action Plan sheet.

- Read about Kathy and her problems at the start of the school year.
- Are your weekday mornings sometimes like Kathy's?
- Do you think the comic strip describes common problems for teens?
- Discuss these **issues** with your partner and then share your ideas with the class.

Word Wise

I can relate to Kathy because ...
I have the same problem when ...
A lot of students are ...
Most students don't ...

Glossary

taming the stress monster = eliminating stress
issues = problems, subjects
coined = invented
dragged on = seemed to last a long time
wiped = extremely tired
I can't wait = I am very impatient

Energy In, Energy Out

How well you sleep and eat can affect your energy levels. Energy in ... energy out!

FYI

Benjamin Franklin first **coined** the expression "Early to bed and early to rise makes a man healthy, wealthy and wise" back in the 18th century!

First

- Explore the text by looking at the title and subtitles.
- Write down one question that you think will be answered in the text.

Next

- Read the text and look for the answer to your question.
- Use resources to understand new words.

STRATEGY

- **Skim** the text to quickly get a general idea of the subject.
- **Scan** the text to look for specific information and the answers to questions.

- Read the text again and answer these questions:
  - What are three negative effects of sleep deprivation?
  - What are three positive effects of a good night's sleep?

Finally

- What did you find most interesting in the article?
- Discuss these questions with a partner and then with the whole class:

  Which of the tips on page 17
  - work for you already?
  - could work for you?
  - are totally unrealistic?
- Add some notes to your Action Plan.

Glossary

drags his ... body = forces himself to go
slip = go down rapidly
counteract = neutralize
avoid (exercising) = try not (to exercise)

Getting Enough Sleep?

TEENS SLEEPING

By Charlotte Doran

It's late September and Marc gets up at 7 a.m. He **drags his** sleepy **body** to school. Marc has a classic case of sleep deprivation. He is not alone. Studies show that most teenagers do not get
5 enough sleep. With less than 8½ hours of sleep, teens often see their school grades **slip** because their brains are not getting the rest they need. Not getting enough sleep also means that they might be irritable and impatient with the people
10 around them.

Word Wise

I already ...
I could ...
This would not work for me because ...
I think tip number (1) could work for me.

THROUGH THEIR SCHOOL YEARS

This graph shows some of the results of a recent poll conducted by the National Sleep Foundation.

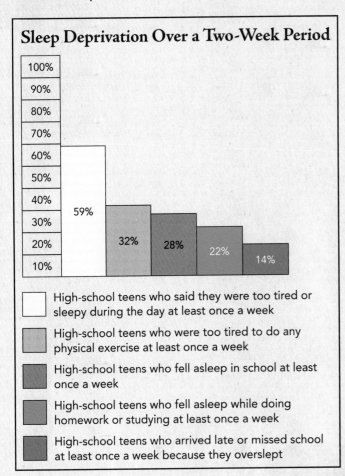

Sleep Deprivation Over a Two-Week Period

- 100%
- 90%
- 80%
- 70%
- 60%
- 50%
- 40%
- 30%
- 20%
- 10%

59% 32% 28% 22% 14%

High-school teens who said they were too tired or sleepy during the day at least once a week

High-school teens who were too tired to do any physical exercise at least once a week

High-school teens who fell asleep in school at least once a week

High-school teens who fell asleep while doing homework or studying at least once a week

High-school teens who arrived late or missed school at least once a week because they overslept

The well-rested brain

To **counteract** the negative effect of sleep
5 deprivation, some schools start later in the morning. Teens with well-rested brains usually have an easier time remembering details. They are generally more creative and have a more positive attitude. This makes life easier for everybody,
10 especially the students.

Sleep experts offer tips for teens

1. Try to go to sleep and wake up at the same time every day, even on weekends.
2. Make sure there is no light in your bedroom
15 when sleeping. Your brain needs darkness to relax and prepare for the next day.
3. Physical exercise during the day helps you sleep at night. **Avoid** exercising just before going to bed.
20 4. Do not play video games or watch a dramatic TV program before going to bed.
5. Don't eat big snacks before sleeping and avoid caffeine in the afternoon.
6. Prepare your body and brain for sleep: take a
25 warm bath or read a relaxing book.

GRAMMAR WORKS

Imperatives are used to give instructions, directions, orders and warnings.
- For affirmative statements, use the **base form** of the verb (the infinitive without *to*).
  Make sure …   **Take** a warm bath.
- For negative statements, use **do + not** (or **don't**) + **base form** of the verb.
  Do not play video games …   **Don't eat** big snacks …

Food for Thought

First

- What can a healthy diet do for your brain? Read the text to find out.

Next

- Which of the following breakfasts do you think is the best to start your school day?
  - Cereal, bran muffin, cup of coffee
  - Yogourt, cheese, cereal
  - Toast with peanut butter, cheese, orange juice
  - Omelette, bacon, apple juice
- Explain your choice to your partner.

Finally

- Tell your partner what you usually eat in the morning.

Glossary

kick-start = start quickly
e.g. = for example
enhance = improve, help
harm = hurt, damage

What's in a Word?

- What do you think the expression "food for thought" means?
- Do you know any other expressions about food or eating?

Food affects how your brain functions and helps it make the right connections.

The best way to **kick-start** your brain is to have a good breakfast that includes
5   ✓ calcium (**e.g.** milk, yogourt, cheese)
   ✓ proteins (e.g. eggs, peanut butter)
   ✓ complex carbohydrates (e.g. fruit, juice)

Foods such as vegetables, chickpeas, eggs, beans and fish **enhance** your mental
10 performance—a good idea before a test!

So, does what you eat during the day help you or **harm** you? It's definitely food for thought!

GRAMMAR WORKS

The Simple Present Tense

1 **Show what you know.**

- Find the verbs in the simple present tense in the following text.
- In your notebook, indicate if each verb is in the affirmative form (A) or the negative form (N).

When I eat a healthy breakfast, I have more energy during the day. That is a fact. But I often don't have time for more than an energy bar and a glass of milk. I know, I wake up late because I don't get to bed early enough. Well, it isn't easy. I have so much homework to do and I have basketball practice after school. I need time to relax, too.

2 **Review the simple present tense.**

Affirmative form
- To form the **simple present tense** of most verbs, use the base form of the verb. The third-person singular ends in **s**.

  I **sleep** nine hours every night.   Paul **plays** hockey three nights a week.
  We **eat** a healthy breakfast.   Exercising **improves** concentration.

Negative form
- For negative statements, add **do not (don't)** before the base form of the verb. For the third-person singular, add **does not (doesn't)** before the verb.

  I **do not sleep** well at night.   Janet **doesn't play** any sports.
  We **don't** always **eat** a full breakfast.   He **doesn't get** up on time.

The verb **to be** is an exception.

Affirmative forms		Negative forms	
I **am** sleepy.	I'm ...	I **am not** sleepy.	I'm not ...
You **are** late.	You're ...	You **are not** late.	You **aren't** ...
She **is** hungry.	She's ...	She **is not** hungry.	She **isn't** ...
We **are** tired.	We're ...	We **are not** tired.	We **aren't** ...
They **are** stressed out.	They're ...	They **are not** stressed out.	They **aren't** ...

For more on the simple present tense, go to page 184.

3 **Practise.**

Complete the sentences with the appropriate form of the simple present.

Students who regularly (*to work out*) usually (*to feel*) better about themselves. They (*to become*) more confident. This often (*to lead*) to better class participation and better grades. Even a 20-minute walk (*to be*) a good way to improve your body and your brain if you (*to do*) it two or three times a week. Exercising (*to guarantee, neg.*) you an A+. However, it (*to be*) sure to make you feel better.

The Multi-tasking Teen

How well do you **manage** your time? Are you organized or disorganized? Do you find time to do the things you like? Or are you always running at the last minute, all stressed out?

First

- In your notebook, draw three columns. Follow the example below.
- Read the two case studies on the next page. Take notes of the good and bad habits of each teen. Write them in the first column.
- Compare your notes with a partner. Is there anything you would like to change or add?

What Karl and Stephanie do	What I do now	What I could do
Karl Good: takes notes, rereads notes Bad: puts notes in wrong binder	I take notes sometimes, but my handwriting is terrible so they're hard to read	I could ...

Next

- In the second column, compare your current habits with Karl's and Stephanie's.

Finally

- Fill in the third column with things you could do this year to help you manage your time.
- Add some notes to your Action Plan sheet.

Glossary

manage = organize
wastes time = does not use time efficiently
spends a lot of time = uses a lot of time
assignments = homework, projects
in shape = in good physical condition
mall = indoor shopping centre

CASE STUDIES

Karl T.

At school, Karl tries to pay attention in class and takes a lot of notes. Unfortunately, he forgets to put his notes in the right binder, so he **wastes time** looking for his material. At home, when he finally does find his notes, he rereads them to make
5 sure he understands. After school he plays the saxophone in the school band. He **spends a lot of time** practising every evening. Sometimes he has to rush to do his homework. On the weekends, Karl finishes his homework on Saturday morning. In the afternoon he works cutting grass or shovelling snow for his neighbours. He uses the money to go to the movies and to do other activities he enjoys.
10 Sometimes he comes home late on Sunday, so he is usually tired when he gets up on Monday morning.

Stephanie B.

Stephanie writes all her homework in her agenda. She also colour-codes the dates her projects are due. Stephanie is very artistic. She draws as many pictures as she
15 can all over her agenda. Because of this, it can be difficult to see what work she has to do. She is sometimes late doing her **assignments**. Stephanie is on the Art Committee at school and spends many lunchtimes painting murals in the school corridors. She plays tennis twice a week to keep **in shape** and takes guitar lessons every Friday evening. On Saturdays she goes to the **mall** with her friends.
20 Stephanie does most of her homework on Sunday night while she watches TV. She gets stressed out before exams because she often doesn't have enough time to study.

VOCABULARY

GRAMMAR WORKS

In the **simple present tense**, the third-person singular ends in **s**.

takes   forgets   plays

Add **es** to verbs that end in **ch**, **sh**, **o**, **s**, **x** or **z**.

does   finishes   watches

Change the **y** to **ies** when the verb ends in a <u>consonant</u> + y.

tries   studies

Just Laugh It Off

First

- With a partner read the three jokes. Match the **punchline** to each joke.
- Which joke did you find the funniest? The least funny?

It's important not to let school stress you out. One of the best ways to relax is to laugh a little.

①
Teacher: Your dog ate your homework?

Student: Yes, Miss.

Teacher: And where is your dog now?

Student: [punchline]

②
Student: Sir, would you punish someone for something they didn't do?

Teacher: Of course not.

Student: [punchline]

③
Student: I didn't come to school this morning because I got up too late.

Teacher: Why didn't you get up earlier?

Student: [punchline]

Punchlines

A It was too late to get up early.

B At the **vet's**. It doesn't like homework either.

C That's good. I didn't do my homework last night.

Next

- Read about three embarrassing experiences.
- Which one would you find the most embarrassing?
- Which is the funniest?

Glossary

punchline = final line of a joke
vet's = veterinarian's office
tackles = attempts to stop him
score a touchdown = reach the end zone and win points
bumps (into) = hits, collides (with)

Embarrassing or Funny?

Sometimes embarrassing situations make us want to run and hide but they can also be pretty funny—especially if they happen to somebody else!

① You are playing football on a new team. You want to prove yourself and show off your talent. In the middle of the game, you finally get hold of the ball. You feel great! You run, avoid several **tackles** and then you **score a touchdown** … for the wrong team!

② You are walking in the cafeteria with a tray full of food: a bowl of soup, a plate of spaghetti, grape juice and pudding. You are hurrying to the table where all of your friends are sitting. Suddenly, you slip on a banana peel. The tray goes flying and you end up lying on the floor, covered with food.

③ Your father drives you to school. As he pulls up in front of the school, he is distracted by a call on his cell phone and **bumps** into the car in front of him. You jump out to see who is in the other car. It turns out to be a woman and her daughter, the girl you were going to ask out on a date!

⊙ ASK YOURSELF…
What do you think now?

Reread all your notes on your Action Plan sheet. Do you want to add anything? Remember that one of the questions was "What can you do to avoid stress and have a more enjoyable year?" Add some notes in part 2.

LANGUAGE WORKS

Opinions, Advice and Feedback

1 **Look at the following language models.**

I think she could …	I agree with …
He needs to …	I totally disagree with …
She should try to …	What do you think?
In my opinion, …	I don't think so.

2 **Form teams.**

- Practise using the language models. Use your imagination to complete the sentences in the box.

3 **Listen to the conversation.** 🎧

- Some students are talking about Marianne. She has problems organizing her time.
- Pay attention to the language they use to express opinions and to give advice or feedback.
- Write down a few examples as you listen.

4 **Give some advice.**

- Read the four situations on page 25.
- Discuss ways to help each student. Look through the unit for ideas.

STRATEGY

Remember you can use strategies to aid communication. See pages 205–207 for a complete list of strategies.

Glossary

drop = go down quickly
running errands = doing tasks, going to the store
give it up = stop doing it
hangs out = spends time
rushes through = does it in a hurry

SITUATION 1

Kayla studies all the time. She is on the school newspaper team. It takes up a lot of her time. She constantly worries that her grades will **drop**. She babysits on Friday evenings and works at the local corner store on Saturdays. When she has time, she goes to the movies with her friends on Saturday evenings. On Sundays and weeknights, after studying and doing homework, she has very little time to relax, so she doesn't sleep well.

SITUATION 2

Anne-Marie is involved in the Student Council. She has meetings at lunchtime and after school twice a week. She spends a lot of time preparing for her meetings and has problems finding the time to study. Anne-Marie also volunteers at the local community centre. She is always busy doing something different: **running errands** for elderly people or painting the community hall.

SITUATION 3

Patrick has football practice three nights a week and a game on the weekend. He finds it difficult to keep up with his school work but loves football too much to **give it up**. During the weekend, after the game, he **hangs out** with his friends and watches TV. Because he does not spend a lot of time on his homework, he finds it difficult to understand in class.

SITUATION 4

Karim gets out of bed at the last minute and has to run for the school bus. By lunchtime, he is starving and exhausted. He drinks a can of soda and eats some fries to get him through the afternoon. When he gets home, he **rushes through** his homework so he can watch his favourite TV shows. He never misses a hockey game. On weekends he plays video games with friends. He loves to chat online until late at night.

VOCABULARY

SELF-CHECK

☑ Think about the strategies you used. Which ones were most helpful to you? Which ones will you try to use the next time you interact orally?

Write On

◎ YOUR TASK

Write a text about what you can do to avoid stress and have a more enjoyable year.

Your text will contain:
- an opening statement
- a separate paragraph detailing your intentions for each aspect (sleep, food, etc.)
- a conclusion that summarizes your main intentions ————————

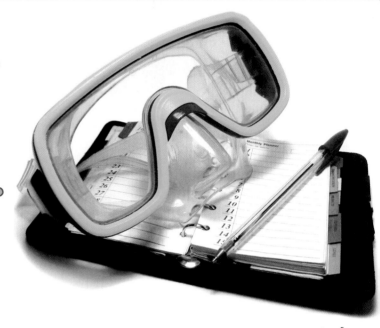

1 Plan your work.

- Look at the model on page 27. Use the same structure for your text.
- Think about the things you learned in the unit about sleep, nutrition, exercise and time management.
- Think about what you already do and what you could do.
- Look at your notes on your Action Plan sheet for ideas.
- Use a graphic organizer to organize your thoughts.

2 Write a first draft of your text.

- Look at your graphic organizer to help you write about the different aspects.
- Use new words from your vocabulary log.

3 Revise and edit your text.

- Add, substitute, delete and rearrange ideas and words.
- Add a title to your text.
- Edit your text using your checklist and other resources as needed.
- Ask someone to check your work.
- Write your final copy.

4 Go public.

- Share your text with the class.

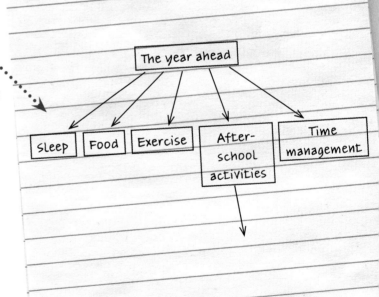

The year ahead

Sleep | Food | Exercise | After-school activities | Time management

MY PERSONAL PLAN

By Patrick St-Pierre

OPENING STATEMENT

There are some things I can do this year to have more fun and be less stressed out. There are also some things I am not prepared to do ...

DETAILS ABOUT INTENTIONS

First of all, I can ... But I need ...

Secondly, I know I can't always ... But I could try to ...

Finally, I think that I could ...

CONCLUSION

So, in conclusion, I have three main intentions I plan to ...

Wish me luck!

VOCABULARY

UNIT 3

Project: Poster Power

eating well

⊚ ANSWER THIS ...

In the past two units, you examined ways to make your life more enjoyable and stress-free. In your opinion, what is the most important issue facing Secondary III students?

What advice would you give them through the medium of a poster? ————————○

making friends

working part-time in the evening

dealing with stress

finding time for homework

With a classmate, talk about the issues listed on this page.

- Which issue do you think is the most important?
- Which ones are problematic for you?
- Do you have solutions to suggest?

WOrd Wise

That's a major problem for me.
I have a solution for that.
That's not really a problem for me.
... is an important issue because ...

YOUR PROJECT

Decide on an issue you want to address and what advice you want to give in poster form. Present your project to the class.

- Think about these questions.
  1. Where do you usually see posters?
  2. What kinds of posters do you see?
  3. What characteristics do they have?
  4. What sort of messages do they contain?

- Here is what communications specialists have to say about effective posters.

- Do the posters you see around you have these characteristics?

CHARACTERISTICS OF AN EFFECTIVE POSTER

Design
- An effective poster is easy to read.
- Its design is well organized.

Impact
- People notice it and want to read it.
- People want to talk about it.

Message
- Its message is clear.
- The words and pictures reinforce the message.

Deconstructing Posters

First

- Look carefully at the posters on pages 30, 31 and 32.
- Analyze the posters. For each poster answer these questions.
  1. What grabs your attention?
  2. What do you think of the pictures?
  3. Is there a balance between pictures and text?
  4. What is the central message?
  5. Who is the intended audience?
  6. Is the message appropriate for the intended audience?

POSTER 1　Smoking

Secondhand Smoke
is dangerous to children

Smoking around children can cause sudden infant death syndrome (SIDS), lung problems, ear infections, and more severe asthma.

Secondhand smoke
It hurts you. It doesn't take much. It doesn't take long.

Glossary

It doesn't take much. = It can easily happen.

It doesn't take long. = It can happen very fast.

wipes = packaged cleaning tissues

overloaded = too full, stuffed

spine = backbone, vertebral column

misalignment = distortion

straps = strips of cloth or leather used to carry something

snug = tight but comfortable

USE A TISSUE

BE A GERM STOPPER.

COVER MOUTH AND NOSE

CLEAN HANDS

Cover Coughs and Sneezes. Clean Hands.

Be a germ stopper at school — and home. Cover your mouth and nose when you cough or sneeze. Use a tissue and throw it away.

Clean your hands a lot
- After you sneeze or cough
- After using the bathroom
- Before you eat
- Before you touch your eyes, mouth or nose

Washing hands with soap and water is best. Wash long enough to sing the "Happy Birthday" song twice. Or, use gels or wipes with alcohol in them. This alcohol kills germs!

Stop germs. And stop colds and flu.

www.cdc.gov/germstopper

BACKPACK SAFETY INTERNATIONAL™

YOU CAN DO IT.

Just do it right!

©2004

WRONG

This backpack is over-loaded, creating stress on the spine. Improper backpack use can lead to a lifetime of health problems.

WRONG

Wearing a backpack improperly over one shoulder can cause permanent misalignment of the spine, muscle fatigue, and a lowered state of health.

4 STEPS TO SAFE BACKPACK USE

1 CHOOSE RIGHT

Choosing the correct size backpack is the most important step to safe backpack use.

TIP: Bring a friend to help you measure your backpack properly.

2 PACK RIGHT

The maximum weight of the loaded backpack should not exceed 15% of your body weight, so pack only what is needed.

TIP: If the backpack forces the wearer to bend forward to carry, it's overloaded.

3 LIFT RIGHT

• Face the pack.
• Bend at the knees.
• Use both hands and check the weight of the pack.
    • Lift with the legs.
    • Apply one shoulder strap then the other.

TIP: Don't sling the backpack onto one shoulder.

4 WEAR RIGHT

Use both shoulder straps – snug, but not too tight.

TIP: When the backpack has a waist strap, use it.

PETE THE POSTURE PARROT
SEAL OF APPROVAL

Then

● With a partner, complete the chart on your activity sheet. Compare your answers.
● Make an overall evaluation of each poster.
● Share your analysis and evaluation of the three posters with another pair of students.

	Poster 1	Poster 2	Poster 3
Analysis of the posters			
1. Does it grab your attention?			
2. Is the design well organized or not?			
3. Is it easy to read?			
4. Do the words and pictures reinforce the message?			
5. Is the message clear or not?			
Evaluation of the posters			
6. Do you like this poster?			
7. Overall evaluation	/10	/10	

WOrd Wise

This poster is …
The pictures are …
The text is …
very well done
dynamic
well chosen
powerful
not attractive / clear / catchy
difficult / easy to understand

Finally

● Together, decide which of the three is the most effective poster.
● Be prepared to explain the reasons for your choice.

Producing a Poster

① PREPRODUCTION

● **Plan your project.**

- With a partner, choose an issue that is important to Secondary III students. Find advice that can help make their year more enjoyable and stress-free. ⋯⋯⋯⋯►
- Get ideas for content from Units 1 and 2.
- If computers are available, search the Internet for topics and poster design ideas.
- Refer to page 29 for the characteristics of effective posters.
- Decide on the essential message.
- Decide what tasks you and your partner will do (research, pictures, text, layout, revision, etc.).

② PRODUCTION

● **Prepare a first draft.**

- Write the first draft.
- Choose effective vocabulary. Write powerful statements to get the essential message across to your audience.
- Decide on a portrait (▮) or landscape (▬) poster.
- Try different arrangements for your texts and pictures.
- Choose colours and fonts. ⋯⋯⋯⋯⋯⋯►
- Show your draft to another pair of students. Use their feedback to make adjustments.

ISSUES

- study habits
- making friends
- sleep habits
- homework strategies
- eating habits
- regular exercise
- time management
- stress management
- using your senses to relax
- other

REMEMBER

Effective projects depend on
- teamwork
- careful planning
- creative ideas
- doing tasks on time
- dynamic presentation

Media Alert

Use light pastel colours for the background.
Use darker colours for contrast.
Use fonts that are large enough to read at a distance.

What's in a Word?

- Use words like *exciting* instead of *nice*.
- Use powerful statements like "Stop eating junk food!" instead of "Eat well."

- **Make the final version of your poster.**
  - Create the poster, taking the feedback from your classmates into account.
  - Revise and edit your texts carefully.
  - Make sure that the essential message can be easily understood.
  - If computers are available, use software to produce a polished product.
  - Ask yourself: Will this poster make the audience take this issue seriously?

❸ POSTPRODUCTION

- **Present your poster to the class.**
  - Share the tasks of doing the presentation.
  - Make your presentation as dynamic and memorable as possible.

> **STRATEGY**
>
> Which strategies will help you with your presentation?
> See pages 205–207 in the Reference section.

  - State why you chose the topic for your presentation.
  - Solicit reactions from the class about the issue.

- **Reflect on the project.**
  - Think back about what you learned in this unit and the production process you used.

WOrd Wise

What do you think of our poster?
What suggestions can you make for improving it?
What is our poster's message?
Do you agree or disagree with the message?

Glossary

unveil = show for the first time

TIPS FOR DYNAMIC PRESENTATIONS

- Articulate clearly and with enthusiasm. Sell it!
- Don't stay frozen in one place. Move around.
- Use gestures.
- **Unveil** the poster at the appropriate time, like after your introduction.
- Point to the part of the poster that you are talking about.
- Take turns with your partner while presenting the poster.
- Ask the audience questions to find out what they think of the topic.
- Smile.

UNIT 4

Hot! Hot! Hot!

ASK YOURSELF ...

What do you know about global warming? What are its causes? What can be done to slow down global warming? Write down your ideas about these questions on your Action Plan sheet. ———○

- With a partner, read the five statements on the environment and decide whether they are true or false.
- Come to a consensus.
- You can check your answers by looking through the unit.
- Then, look at the pictures on the next page. Can you identify some of these phenomena? Look at the Word Wise list for clues.
- Which pictures show possible causes of global warming? Which pictures show its effects?

Glossary

global warming = the increase in the Earth's temperature caused by the increase in certain gases
greenhouse gas = gases that are trapped in the atmosphere
fossil fuels = coal, oil, natural gas

What Do I Know?

We hear a lot about global warming and issues concerned with the environment. Try this quiz to see how well informed you are.

True or False?

1. Scientists only became aware of **global warming** at the end of the 20th century.

2. The average surface temperature of the earth is 18°C.

3. Transportation is responsible for more than a quarter of Canada's total **greenhouse gas** emissions.

4. Most of our energy comes from **fossil fuels**.

5. The hole in the ozone layer is caused by ultraviolet rays.

Word Wise

This picture shows ...
air pollution
destruction of natural habitats
drought
flooding
garbage
hurricane
ice storm
industrial waste
water pollution
... could be a cause of global warming.
... could be an effect of global warming.

First

- Work alone on the text *Warning! Warning!*
- Use resources to understand new words.
- Read the text and complete the reading log.
- As you read, fill in each section of the graphic organizer with information from the text.

STRATEGY

Organize information.
Using a graphic organizer will help you to understand the text.

Next

- Compare your notes with a partner. Is there anything you would like to change or add?

Finally

- Share your information with the class.
- What did you learn from the text?

Glossary

in hot water = in serious trouble
layer = cover, coat
hot topics = popular subjects
consumption = usage
CFCs = chlorofluorocarbons
in the hot seat = in a difficult position, under pressure
putting the heat on = pressuring, demanding action

What's in a Word?

IN HOT WATER   HOT TOPICS   IN THE HOT SEAT   PUT THE HEAT ON
These "hot" expressions draw attention to the fact that global warming is an important and controversial subject. Look for them in the text. See the glossary for their meaning.

In Hot Water?

The earth's temperature has increased by 0.75°C over the last 100 years. What does that mean for us? Is our planet in trouble?

Warning! Warning!

The greenhouse effect, global population, the ozone **layer** are all **hot topics** these days. Global warming is on everybody's mind.

One big greenhouse

5 A greenhouse is a glass house that traps heat from the sun. Greenhouses are used to cultivate plants, especially in winter. The hot rays from the sun pass through the glass panels, heating the air inside. The hot air cannot escape and the warm
10 environment helps the plants to grow.

Just like a greenhouse, the Earth's atmosphere traps heat from the sun near the planet's surface. This is called the greenhouse effect. This heat is keeping the Earth's average temperature at 15°C.
15 Without the greenhouse effect, the average temperature of our world would be around -18°C. On the other hand, if the temperature of the Earth increases just a little, it could mean disaster. A very small rise in temperature could lead to drought in
20 some areas and flooding in others. ⬤

More people

The global population has doubled since 1960 and will probably reach nine billion by 2050. More people means more energy **consumption**.
25 Most of our energy comes from fossil fuels such as coal, oil and natural gas. Fossil fuels release gases, particularly carbon dioxide, into the atmosphere. These gases are trapping too much heat from the sun, causing the earth to warm
30 up. Most scientists feel that climatic changes around the world may be the consequence of global warming. ⬤

Less protection

The ozone layer is a 20-kilometre layer of gas that
35 is found high above the Earth's surface. It protects the Earth from the sun's harmful ultraviolet (UV) rays. In the 1980s, a hole was found in the ozone layer. As a result, we have less protection from the sun and more UV rays are reaching the earth.
40 This could mean an increase in the number of people suffering from skin cancers and cataracts.

Scientists believe that the hole is caused by **CFCs** in the stratosphere. CFCs are chemicals found in old refrigerators and in some car air conditioners
45 and aerosol propellants. Fortunately, thanks to international agreements like the 1987 Montréal Protocol, production of CFCs has stopped in most countries. ⬤

FYI The idea of global warming caused by human activities was first introduced by Swedish chemist Svante Auguste Arrhenius … in 1897!

In the hot seat

50 Many people are now **putting the heat on** their governments to adopt environmentally friendly laws. They want to reduce the amount of bad gases and chemicals in the air and slow down global warming. ⬤

VOCABULARY

GRAMMAR WORKS

Active or Passive Voice?
- Verbs in the **active voice** indicate that the subject of the sentence **does** the action.
  … the Earth's atmosphere **traps** heat from the sun …
- Verbs in the **passive voice** indicate that the subject of the sentence **receives** the action but does not <u>do</u> the action.
  … the hole **is caused** by CFCs in the stratosphere.
- Passive verbs are made up of the verb **to be** + the **past participle** of the verb.
  Greenhouses **are used** to cultivate plants …

Hot Transportation Solutions

More and more people are on the move in the world and this has an impact on our environment.

First

- Think of strategies you can use to understand the text.
- Use resources to understand new words.
- Read the text *Trains, Planes and … Scooters?* Use a graphic organizer to take notes. Follow the example.

Next

- With a partner, compare your answers. If you don't agree, check the text.

Finally

- Tell your partner:
  - what surprised you in the text
  - which mode of transportation you find the most interesting
  - which ecological mode of transportation you would use to go to the following places:
    - school
    - shopping centre
    - sports arena
    - Toronto
    - Florida

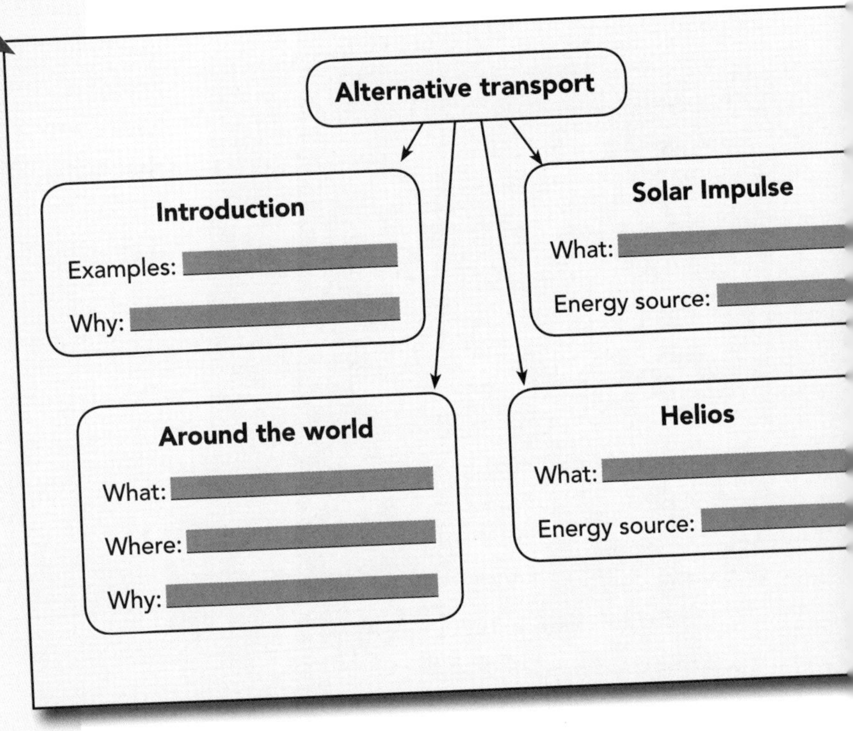

Alternative transport
Introduction
Examples:
Why:
Solar Impulse
What:
Energy source:
Around the world
What:
Where:
Why:
Helios
What:
Energy source:

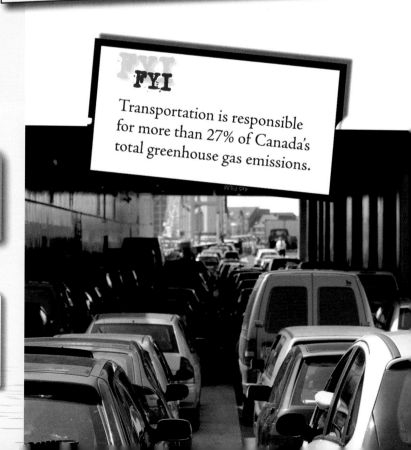

FYI

Transportation is responsible for more than 27% of Canada's total greenhouse gas emissions.

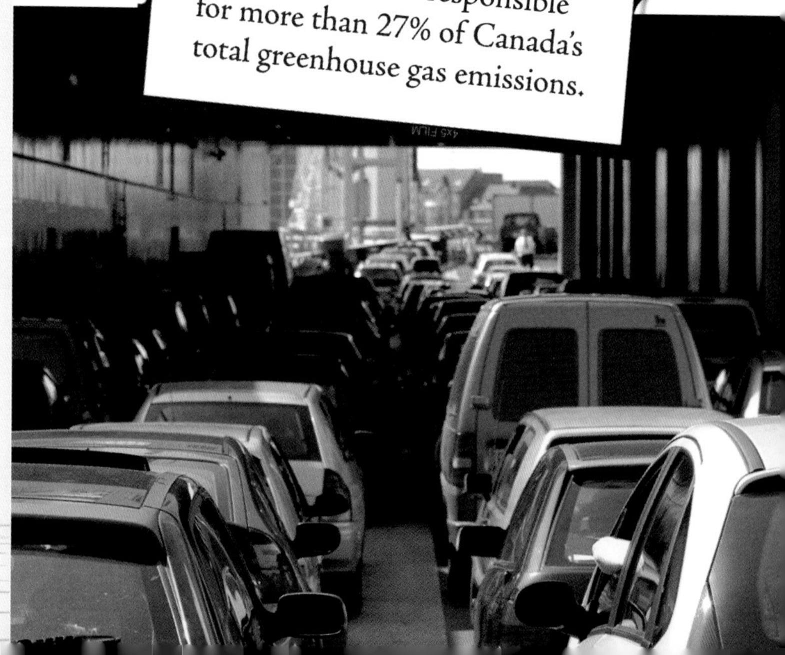

Word Wise

I didn't know that …
I think … is really interesting because …
I would use … because …
I think we should …

Glossary

biogas = gas that comes from organic waste
emit = produce
scoot = hurry
scooter = motorbike
shield = protective cover

Trains, Planes and ... Scooters?

One way to slow down global warming is to change the way we get around. Many people are now walking, biking or using public transportation. Others are trying hard to find more solutions.

Around the world

Many countries are working toward environmentally friendly transport—even trains are being modified. In Sweden, many electric trains are now using **biogas**, hydropower or wind power to operate. This means that
10 the trains **emit** almost no pollutants into the atmosphere. In Japan, they are operating hybrid trains that run on both diesel and batteries. This type of train reduces gas emissions by 60%.

Fly like a bird

15 Swiss explorer Bertrand Picard plans to fly solo around the world—without fuel or pollution! To do this, Picard is developing the Solar Impulse, a lightweight plane that uses solar energy to fly. The solar cells on the plane's very long wings capture solar energy during the day. This
20 energy is used to power the plane's propellers. Extra energy is stored in batteries for night flying. Thanks to Solar Impulse, engineers are learning how to build planes that are lighter and pollute less.

Scoot on over

25 The Helios is the ecological answer to the **scooter**! Developed by Corey Fontaine, an Industrial Design student at Université de Montréal, it runs on high performance batteries. The batteries are plugged in each night and recharged. During the day, three solar panels supply extra
30 energy. When parked, the scooter's sun **shield** becomes a fourth solar panel. Engineers are now looking at solar-powered vehicles as a solution to traffic pollution.

◎ **ASK YOURSELF...**
What do you think now?

Look at the notes you wrote on your Action Plan sheet. Is there anything you would like to change or add? Add some notes in part 2.

VOCABULARY

First

- Work with a partner.
- Look at the cartoons on this page. What do you think they mean?
- Answer the two riddles.

Next

- Read the *True or False* statements on the next page.
- Decide which statements are true and which are false.
- Which facts do you find funny?

Finally

- Read about some not-so-serious weather predictions.
- Tell your partner what you think of the text.

Glossary

get a point across = make people aware of an issue
flies = small flying insects
belch = emit gas from the mouth
biodegrade = decompose
flatulence = digestive gas, farting
accurate = exact, without mistakes

Environmental Humour

Humour is often used to **get a point across**.

"I hate Global Warming!"

Riddle 1

What has four wheels and **flies**?

(A garbage truck)

Riddle 2

What do penguins have for lunch?

(Icebergers)

True or False?

1. Global warming is caused by solar energy.
2. Watching TV or playing video games produces greenhouse gases.
3. Cows and sheep contribute to global warming when they **belch**.
4. Carbon dioxide (CO_2) smells bad.
5. The earth's atmosphere is made up of about 21% CO_2.
6. Plastic bags take from 450 to 1000 years to **biodegrade**.
7. The number of Adele penguins in the Antarctic has gone down by 33% in the past 50 years.
8. Termite **flatulence** is believed to contribute to global warming.

Groundhog Day!

Every year on February 2nd, known as Groundhog Day, people all over Canada await news of a groundhog's predictions about spring weather. In Wiarton, Ontario, the hometown of Canada's official groundhog, there are huge parties and the animal's prediction is broadcast on national news. Reporters and camera crews watch the groundhog's reaction as it comes out of its den. If the groundhog sees its shadow and runs back into its den, cold wintry weather will probably continue. However, if it does not see its shadow and walks around, spring-like weather should soon come. Just how **accurate** is Canada's official groundhog in its weather predictions? Well, over a number of decades, it has only been correct 37% of the time.

The Present Continuous

1 **Show what you know.**

- Read these sentences from the text *Warning! Warning!* on pages 38 and 39: This heat is keeping the Earth's average temperature at 15°C. More UV rays are reaching the earth.

- In your notebook, write down what you notice about the verbs.

2 **Review the present continuous.**

- The present continuous is made up of two parts: the auxiliary verb **to be** + the main verb ending in **ing**.

Affirmative form

(to watch)	I **am watching** a documentary on the environment.
(to build)	He **is building** a hybrid car.

Negative form

(to take)	You **are** <u>**not**</u> **taking** the situation seriously enough.
(to work)	They **are** <u>**not**</u> **working** together to find a solution.

Question forms

Question word	Auxiliary	Subject	Verb+ing	Rest of the sentence
	Are	you	going	to the meeting?
What	is	he	doing	to help the environment?
How	are	they	dealing	with global warming?

- The present continuous is used to show that an action is happening now. The action began before the present time and will continue for some time after the present.
  Carol-Anne **is riding** her bicycle to school.
  The hole in the ozone layer **is getting** bigger.

- The present continuous can also be used to indicate actions that are sure to take place in the future.
  I'**m taking** the bus to the mall tomorrow.
  We **are starting** a new recycling program in our school next year.

- It is important to specify when the action will take place in the future so there is no confusion between the present and the future.

- Some verbs are usually not used in the continuous form:

to like	to want	to know	to believe	to seem
to love	to hate	to need	to understand	to forget

- These discourse markers are often used with the present continuous:

(right) now	this week	for the time being
at the moment	this month	presently
today	this year	currently

For more on the present continuous, go to page 186.

For more on the present continuous, go to page 186.

3 Practise.

A. Go back to the text *Trains, Planes and … Scooters?* on page 41 and find at least four different verbs that are in the present continuous. Write them in your notebook.

B. Look at these pictures. In your notebook, write a question in the present continuous for each picture.
   - Use the vocabulary in the parentheses. The answers will help you write the questions.
   - Look at the example.

Example:

Question?
(to heat up, the earth)
<u>Why is the Earth heating up?</u>
Answer: Because there is too much pollution.

1. Question?
(you, to heat, your house)
Answer: With solar energy.

2. Question?
(she, to recycle)
Answer: Paper.

3. Question?
(they, to take, the bus)
Answer: Because they want to reduce air pollution.

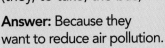

4. Question?
(vehicle, he, to drive)
Answer: A scooter.

5. Question?
(problem, we, to discuss)
Answer: Global warming.

6. Question?
(global warming, to melt, icecaps)
Answer: Yes, it is.

Clarification and Decision-Making

1 **Look at the following language models.**

What do you mean?	Have you come to a decision?
Could you repeat that, please?	What would you decide?
What did you say?	I would decide to …
What I mean is …	It's a difficult decision.
In other words, …	The best decision is …

2 **Form teams.**

- Brainstorm for other language you might use to show something is not clear.

3 **Listen to the conversation.** 🎧

- These students are discussing solutions to the problems that cause global warming.
- Pay attention to the language they use to make a decision and to offer or request clarification.
- Write down a few examples as you listen.

STRATEGY

Remember you can use strategies to aid communication. See pages 205-207 for a complete list of strategies.

4 **Make a decision.**

- With your group, decide which five environmental problems in your school, community or the world are the most important.
- Read the examples on the opposite page.
- Look through the unit for ideas.
- Write the problems on a sheet of paper.
- For each problem, offer at least two solutions.
- Write the solutions below the problems on the sheet of paper.
- Hand your problem–solution sheet to another group.
- Discuss the problems you receive from another group and decide which solutions are the best.

Glossary

spot checks = occasional verifications
household = group of people living in a house
ban = make illegal

Citizens in your community are not recycling or reusing material.

a) Do **spot checks** and give fines to those who do not recycle.
b) Have a competition and give a prize to the family that recycles the most.
c) Limit the amount of regular garbage for each **household**.
d) Make people pay for each bag of garbage they produce.

Some grocery stores are not offering alternatives to plastic bags for groceries.

a) **Ban** all plastic bags in grocery stores.
b) Offer reusable cloth bags at a low price as an alternative to plastic bags.
c) Limit each customer to a maximum of five plastic bags per shopping trip.
d) Make people pay for each plastic bag they take home.

SELF-CHECK

☑ Think about the strategies you used. Which ones were most helpful to you? Which ones will you try to use the next time you interact orally?

Write On

◎ YOUR TASK

Write an article on global warming. Choose an environmental issue that interests you.

Your article will contain
- a strong opening statement or question about the issue
- a separate paragraph for each point or major item of information
- a conclusion that summarizes the major points ────────────○

❶ Plan your writing.

- Look at the text on pages 38–39. Use the same structure for your text.
- Think about the things you learned in this unit about global warming.
- Look at your Action Plan notes for ideas.
- Decide on the issue you want to write about. Choose one of the following topics or suggest another environmental issue:
  - extreme weather and global warming
  - health problems and climate change
  - species endangered by climate change
  - ways to reduce energy use at home
  - my solutions to global warming
- Research your topic at the library and on the Internet.
- Construct an outline of your text.
- Look at the outline model on page 49 to help you structure your text.

❷ Write a first draft of your text.

- Look at your outline to help you write about every important point.
- Use new words from your vocabulary log.
- Go back through the unit for useful language and grammar.

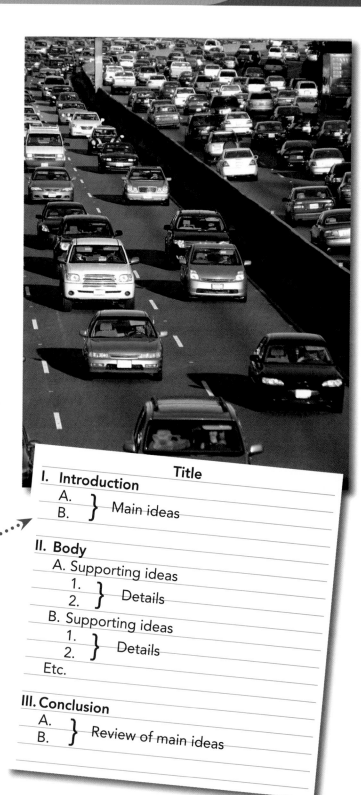

Title

I. **Introduction**
   A.
   B. } Main ideas

II. **Body**
   A. Supporting ideas
      1.
      2. } Details
   B. Supporting ideas
      1.
      2. } Details
   Etc.

III. **Conclusion**
   A.
   B. } Review of main ideas

3 Revise and edit your text.
- Add, substitute, delete and rearrange ideas and words.
- Edit your text, using your checklist and other resources as needed.
- Ask someone to check your work.
- Write your final copy.

4 Go public.
- Share your work with the class.

Gl(O)ssary
catchy = easy to remember
seeps = leaks, escapes

OUTLINE FOR
The Hot Question of Electronic Waste

A. People throw away 140,000 tonnes of electronic waste every year. Danger → for us and the environment
B. Solutions?

A. We throw away computers → mercury **seeps** out
  1. affects our health → brain damage
  2. bad for environment → mercury in soil

B. We throw away cellphones → plastic incinerated
  1. emits gases into atmosphere → adds to global warming
  2. global warming → bad for our health

C. Solutions → recycle
  1. Government program → recycle computers in schools
  2. Private companies → recycle cell phones in developing countries

A. Problems of electronic waste → computers and cell phones
B. Solutions → recycling for a good cause

5 Good Fads, Bad Fads

○ ASK YOURSELF ...

What do you think of fads? Why do people follow fads? Does following fads make a person popular? Write down your ideas about these questions on your Action Plan sheet. ———○

- Look at the pictures. Match the fad names to the correct pictures.
- Guess the decade in which the fads first became popular.
- Share your answers with the class. Say what helped you guess the decade.
- As a class, decide which fads were good and which ones were not.
- Can you think of any similar fads that are popular today?

> Good fads are those you wish would stay forever. Bad fads are those you wish would go away and never come back!

WOrd Wise

I think it's the (1970s) because ...
I still like ...
I think ...
   ... was a great idea.
   ... were absurd.
   ... was just bizarre.
   ... are still popular.

GlOssary

fads = fashions, activities or objects that are extremely popular for a short time

Good or Bad?

How much do you know about these **fads** and when they first became popular?

Ⓐ

○	○	○
The 1920s	The 1930s	The 1940

Ⓑ

Fads

footbags   pole sitting
granny glasses   sideburns
the jitterbug   tattoos
pet rocks   zoot suits

The 1950s   The 1960s   The 1970s   The 1980s   The 1990s

First

- Scan the introduction to discover the main characteristics of a fad. What are they? ....

Next

- In your notebook, draw a timeline from 1920 to 1990 like the one on pages 50 and 51.
- Write the correct fad under each decade.

STRATEGY

Infer.
Make an intelligent guess based on the cues in the texts.

- Which words in each text helped you identify the decade?
- Compare your answers with a partner.

Finally

- Decide whether each fad was a good or bad idea.
- Tell your partner which fads should **make a comeback**.

What's in a W🔵rd?

UNSAFE   UNHEALTHY

- When we add the prefix "un" before a word, we change its meaning.
- The prefix "un" means "not."
  unsafe = not safe
  unhealthy = not healthy

Gl🔵ssary

cringe = react negatively
make a comeback = become popular again
in = popular
millennium = a period of 1000 years
all the rage = extremely popular
the Depression = period of economic decline that started in 1929 and lasted several years
crowds = large groups of people
cheer on = encourage vocally
radical = very great, exceptional

Fads Full Circle

Some fads make us laugh and some make us **cringe**, but they are an interesting part of our culture. Fads quickly become very popular, but most of them do not last very long. Some of the fads from previous decades, such as the platform shoes and bell-bottomed pants of the 1970s, come back into style many years later.

Video arcades

Most video games are now played at home, but several decades ago, the video arcade was the "**in**" place to go. Teens would spend hours at the arcade playing games while listening to music by Madonna and Michael Jackson, popular singers at that time.

Radio shows

Soon after World War I ended, radio shows were very popular. Families sat around their radios and listened to their favorite dramas and comedies, much like we watch TV now. This fad faded out when television was invented a couple of decades later.

Tie-dye T-shirts

These brightly coloured T-shirts with concentric patterns were very popular with hippies during the decade of peace and love. People took plain T-shirts and tied and dyed them at home. The shirts were inexpensive to produce and each pattern was unique.

In-line skates

In-line skates replaced traditional roller skates. Everywhere you looked, people were in-line skating in the parks, on the streets and the sidewalks. This new recreational sport reached its greatest popularity as people were getting ready for the **millennium**.

Ant farms

In the decade following World War II, it was **all the rage** for people to have their own personal ant farms. Real ants were put with some earth in a glass case. The glass made it possible to see the ants interact and move around in their tunnels. People found it relaxing to watch the ants while listening to the music of the very popular Elvis Presley.

Stamp collecting

Collecting stamps was very popular during **the Depression** when people had little money to spend. Because stamp collecting was inexpensive, it was the perfect pastime.

Platform shoes

These high-heeled shoes were popular during the disco period. Platform shoes were available in many styles. The heels usually measured more than five centimeters. Because it was difficult to walk in these shoes, many people were treated for twisted ankles.

Swallowing goldfish

This crazy fad became very popular among college students during World War II. **Crowds** came to **cheer on** the participants. Fortunately, this unsafe and unhealthy fad did not last long.

VOCABULARY

FYI

Some expressions are also fads. Here are some "chat" fads from the past.
"That hairstyle is 'in' this year."
"That CD player is **all the rage.**"
"That game is so **radical!**"

First
- Explore the texts by looking at the pictures. What are the articles about?

Next
- Read the texts carefully. Use strategies and resources.
- As you read, complete the reading log.

Finally
- Which fad do you think is here to stay?
- Which fad do you think is the most sensible?

From Head to Toe

Some fads have strange beginnings. Others change and adapt with time.

Hot head

Many teenagers today wear tuques. In fact, the tuque is often considered Québec's national winter hat. But did you know that women wore the first tuques in the 12th century? By the 16th century, tuques were becoming really popular. Both men and women were putting them on as  a **fashion statement**. By the mid-1800s, many French Canadians in Québec and Ontario were wearing warm knitted tuques very similar to the tuques that are popular today. ●

Wheels on your heels

The very first land skates were invented in the 1700s, but roller skating did not really become popular until the 1950s. In the 1970s, roller discos became **trendy**: young people were dancing on their roller skates to the beat of disco music. Then, in 1986, in-line skates became the new fad. It seemed that nearly everyone was taking to the streets and enjoying the ride. Now, many teens are wearing roller shoes, sneakers with wheels in the heel of the shoe. Some say that roller shoes may be bad for your health, but that doesn't stop this fad from growing. ●

Hip-hop cool

Wearing pants far below the waistline is a fad popular among teenage boys. But where did this fashion trend come from? Believe it or not, it started in prisons. While prisoners were **serving their time**, they wore badly fitting prison uniforms. They were not allowed to use belts to keep their pants up. This style was part of their tough-guy image. It became fashionable in big cities when hip-hop fashion and "gangsta rap" became all the rage in the 1990s. ●

FYI
The town of La Tuque in the province of Québec was named after a rock formation on the river bank that looked like a tuque.

Glossary
fashion statement = stylish clothing
trendy = popular
serving their time = spending time in prison

- Look at the three teenagers.
- Do you think they are fashion victims? Give reasons for your answer.
- Look at their clothes and accessories. Which do you think will make a comeback? Which, in your opinion, should never make a comeback?
- Can you guess in which decade these styles became a fad?
- Complete the activity sheet and compare your answers with a partner.

Fashion Victims

Fashion victims are people who always wear the latest "in" clothes and accessories. They follow all of the fashion fads of a given time very closely, even if the style does not suit them.

A

B

C

First

- Read the magazine editor's blog on the next page.
- Do you agree or disagree with what Elizabeth wrote?

Next

- Share your reaction to the blog with a partner. Give reasons to support your ideas.
- Read the blog responses.
- Decide which express a positive reaction and which express a negative reaction to the interview.
- Write your reaction to the blog response of your choice.

Magazine Editor's Blog

Blogging on the Internet has become a fad. A blog is like a journal of personal thoughts and comments that is available online. Read what the editor of a teen magazine wrote in her blog about teenagers and fads. Then, check out some people's opinions about her ideas.

Glossary

current = happening now
commercials = radio, TV or Internet advertisements

GRAMMAR WORKS

- An adjective is a word that modifies or describes a noun.
  ... **personal** thoughts   People are **curious** ...

- An adjective can also modify or describe a pronoun.
  They are **great** ...   She is **right**.

- In English, adjectives do not vary according to gender and number.
  They are **great** ...   It's **great** ...

- Possessive adjectives in English refer to the possessor, not the thing.
  ... **my** job   ... **my** friends   ... **our** society

A teen magazine editor's blog

April 14

I am often asked about my job. People are curious about what I do and how I get to understand what teenagers like and don't like. Well, I have three teenagers of my own and I like spending time with them at the mall, sporting arenas or festivals. As a magazine editor, I have to be on the lookout for all the latest fads. What's funny is that some of the **current** fads were also popular when I was young. Teenagers might think all their fads are new, but some are really just old fads that are modernized. I think fads are fun. It's interesting to see how they are advertised. Companies still use **commercials** and ads to sell products. But I really think the best way to get teenagers to notice and use new products is through word of mouth and the Internet. I am often asked whether I think teens care about fads. I hope they do. Fads say something about the type of society we live in and our culture. Honestly, I think everybody likes fads and follows them to a certain degree. They are great, especially when we look back and laugh at the good ones and the not-so-good ones.

Posted by: Elizabeth on April 14 at 10:15 AM
VIEW COMMENTS (5) l ADD COMMENT l TRACKBACKS (X) l

The following are examples of comments in response to the blog.

I don't think I am influenced by fads at all. I do my own thing and buy what I want when I want. I don't think this magazine editor can generalize, even if she does have teenagers of her own.
Posted by: Jerome on May 24 at 10:40 PM

I think it's great that the editor believes that young people are not always influenced by companies and their advertising techniques. She is right. I would rather listen to my friends talk about a new product than a TV commercial.
Posted by: Amanda on June 15 at 4:02 PM

I think fads are great! Why do we have to act like we are not influenced by them when we are ... and it's okay! I agree with Elizabeth!
Posted by: Pierre on June 27 at 12:23 PM

I think the editor is wrong when she says we will buy more things online. I prefer going to the shopping centre and hanging out with my friends instead of staring at a computer screen.
Posted by: Jenny on June 28 at 11:54 AM

I don't appreciate the fact that Elizabeth thinks teenagers don't know if a fad is new or not! I know that platform shoes were popular when my mother was young. I read books and watch TV. I don't need to be born in the 1970s to know that bell-bottom pants were first popular then!
Posted by: Max on August 4 at 11:02 PM

⊚ ASK YOURSELF...

VOCABULARY

What do you think now?

Look at the notes you wrote on your Action Plan sheet. Have you changed your mind about any of your answers? Do you have any new ideas or impressions? Write them down in part 2. ———————●

The Simple Past and the Past Continuous

❶ Show what you know.

- Read the following blog.
- Make a T-chart in your notebook.
- List the verbs in the simple past tense on one side and the verbs in the past continuous on the other.

Simple past	Past continuous
came	was blaring

OMG! The other day when I came home from shopping, my favourite CD was **blaring away**. When I went into the living room, my dad was dancing and singing. Then my mom entered the room. She was wearing these cool bell-bottom pants. My jaw dropped! They were just like the pair that I was wearing. My parents looked at each other and laughed. They said that the group on the CD was very popular when they were teenagers. Mom said that the pants reminded her of the pair she wore when she was younger. I didn't know I had that much in common with my parents. Now, there's a scary thought.

Posted by: Shirley on May 20 at 12:24 PM

❷ Review the simple past.

- Use the simple past to describe a completed action in the past.
  Charles and Meagan went to the drive-in theatre yesterday.

Affirmative form

- To form the **simple past** of regular verbs add **d** or **ed** to the base form of the verb.
  My mother like**d** rock music when she was younger.
  Last night we talk**ed** about our favourite groups.

- Irregular verbs change form. For a list of irregular verbs, see page 190.
  Rebecca **bought** a mood ring.
  We **sang** an old song from the 1980s.

Negative form

- For negative statements, add **did not (didn't)** before the base form of the verb.
  There is no difference between regular and irregular verbs.
  Peter **did not like** long sideburns.
  Jennifer **didn't get** a tattoo.

For more on the simple past tense, go to page 187.

❸ Practise.

- Use the simple past to write a blog about what you did over the weekend. Mention at least five activities. Give details.

Glossary
OMG = Oh, my goodness
blaring away = playing very loudly

4 Review the past continuous.

- The past continuous is made up of two parts: the simple past of the verb **to be** + the main verb ending in **ing**.

  Affirmative form
  (to wear)   People **were wearing** roller skates as they danced to disco music.

  Negative form
  (to dance)   Teens **were not dancing** to rap music in 1970.

- Use the past continuous to describe an action that was in progress at a specific moment in the past: We **were skating** around the roller rink when our friends arrived.

- Use the past continuous to show that two actions were happening simultaneously in the past: My brother **was listening** to hip-hop music while I **was playing** video games.

- Remember that some verbs are usually not used in the continuous form:
  - verbs of the senses: *to hear, to see, to smell, to taste*
  - verbs that express feelings or emotions: *to like, to love, to hate, to need, to want, to respect*
  - verbs that express a mental attitude or perception: *to forget, to know, to understand, to believe, to seem, to remember, to think*

For more on the past continuous, go to page 191.

5 Practise.

A. Go back to the text *From Head to Toe* on page 54 and find five examples of verbs in the past continuous.

B. Complete these sentences, using the simple past or the past continuous. See the simple past of irregular verbs on page 190 in the Reference section.

1. While Julie was phoning me, I (*to send*) her a text message.
2. They were going to the video arcade when I (*to meet*) them.
3. Mathew (*to practise*) flips on his skateboard when I arrived.
4. Lucy and I (*to chat*) in the cafeteria when I noticed her mood ring.
5. When my dad (*to be*) younger, he wore tie-dye T-shirts and headbands.

LANGUAGE WORKS

Teamwork and Encouragement

1 Look at the following language models.

Getting started	**Making sure you understand the activity**
Would you like to ...?	What does this word mean?
Who wants to take notes?	What are we supposed to do?
During the activity	**Giving encouragement and praise**
Do we all agree?	That's a good point.
Whose turn is it?	That's a great idea.

2 Form teams.

- Brainstorm for other expressions for teamwork and giving encouragement.

3 Listen to the conversation. 🎧

- These students are talking about things they want or need.
- Pay attention to the use of expressions for teamwork and giving encouragement.
- Write down some examples as you listen.

4 Talk about wants and needs.

- Make and label a chart like this one.
- Look at the list of items. Decide whether each item is a need or a want for you. Place the item in your chart. Write two reasons for your choice.

With your team:
- Share your answers. Give at least one reason for your choice.
- Make a common list of all of your team's needs.
- Place them in order of importance.
- Decide which of the items are fads.
- Why do you consider them fads?

> **STRATEGY**
>
> Remember you can use strategies to aid communication. See pages 205–207 for a complete list of strategies.

need	want	because

Want or need?
- bottled water
- car
- digital camera
- USB key
- college/university education
- designer running shoes
- TV with the latest features
- latest style of jeans
- cellular phone
- high-speed Internet
- laptop computer

> **SELF-CHECK**
>
> ✔ Think about the strategies you used. Which ones were most helpful to you? Which ones will you try to use the next time you interact orally?

Write On

◎ YOUR TASK

Write a blog about fads. Explain what you think of fads and why you think people follow fads. Does following fads make a person popular?

Your article will contain
- your thoughts and opinions about fads and why people follow them
- personal anecdotes or examples using the simple past tense ————————○

I think fads are …

In my opinion, people follow …

Some of the fads I like aren't new. My dad wore …

When I was younger, I …

Now I don't mind spending money on …

So, fads …

———

Posted by: Justin, on October 27 at 2:20 PM

❶ Plan your writing.

- Look at the blog on page 57. Use the same structure for your text.
- Think about personal anecdotes and examples to support your ideas.
- Look at your notes on your Action Plan sheet for ideas.
- Take notes to organize your main ideas.

❷ Write a first draft of your text.

- Look at your notes to help you write about each point.
- Use new words from your vocabulary log.

❸ Revise and edit your text.

- Add, substitute, delete and rearrange ideas and words.
- Edit your text using your checklist and other resources as needed.
- Verify that you have used the simple past.
- Ask someone to check your work.
- Write your final copy.

❹ Go public.

- Post your blog in the classroom.
- Move around and read the different blogs.
- Choose one and write a response.
- Post your response under the blog you chose.
- Read some of your classmates' responses.

UNIT 6

Project: Brochure Allure

Looking at Environmental Issues

global warming and greenhouse effect

hole in the ozone layer

endangered animal species

overpopulation

pollution

deforestation

fossil fuels

○ ANSWER THIS ...

In the past two units, you looked at some environmental and consumer issues. You saw the impact of global warming on our fragile planet. You also examined your role as a consumer, a shopper targeted by advertising and marketing strategies.

What would you tell other students and adults to help them become environmentally responsible consumers? ─────────○

With a classmate, talk about these issues.

● In your opinion, which of the issues shown on this page are the most important? Choose three.
● Which consumer habits and products cause these issues?
● What can be done?

Word Wise

I think ... are the most important issues.
That's a major issue for me, too.
That causes ...
People could use less ...

◉ YOUR PROJECT

Make a "green" (environmentally friendly) shopping guide for a specific group of consumers. Present your project to the class.

- Think about these questions.
  1. Where do you usually see brochures?
  2. What kinds of brochures do you see?
  3. What characteristics do they have?
  4. What sort of messages do they contain?

- Here are some of the characteristics of a successful brochure.

- Shopping guides target specific consumer groups, such as **tweens,** teens and adults. Here are some of the things they like to buy.

Tweens

Teens

Adults

CHARACTERISTICS OF A SUCCESSFUL BROCHURE

An effective brochure ...

- speaks directly to a specific target audience or consumer group

- uses colours, fonts and images to grab the reader's attention quickly

- focuses on one clear message

- provides useful information in a dynamic manner

- presents advantages and benefits to the reader

- directs the reader to take action

Glossary
tweens = 10 to 12 year olds

First

- Look carefully at the brochure on pages 64 and 65.
- Analyze the brochure. Answer these questions.

The cover page

1. What grabs your attention first?
2. What do you think of the slogan "Compact but amazingly complete!"?
3. What do you think of the photo?

Pages 2, 3 and 4 of the brochure

4. What do you think of the artwork or photos?
5. What does the logo on page 3 of the brochure represent?
6. Who is the brochure written for?
7. Are the language and illustrations suitable for this audience?
8. What do you think of the colours?
9. Are the type size and fonts used for the titles and texts appropriate?
10. Is the text easy to understand?
11. What message is being sent?
12. Do you think the checklist on the last page is helpful to a potential buyer?

In general

13. Does the brochure look professional?
14. Is there anything that you don't like?

Glossary

laptop = portable (computer)
amazingly = surprisingly
stuff = things
fans = components that move air to cool the computer
rivals = is as good as
surround-sound system = sound system with many speakers
gamer = person who loves to play video games

Student Guide to Buying

Laptop Computers*

Compact but amazingly complete!

* also known as notebook computers

cover

Advantages of laptop computers

✦ Laptops are portable. You can literally take them anywhere: your room, school, the beach, a friend's house, etc.

✦ Laptops are compact. They don't need much space—a big advantage when your room is already full of **stuff**.

✦ Laptops are quiet. Their parts are much smaller. Unlike big desktop computers, they don't need noisy **fans** to cool things down.

✦ Laptops are expansible. You can add new technology and software as they become available.

✦ Laptops are now powerful. They have as much memory and operating capacity as desktop computers.

✦ Laptops have great displays. The variety of screen sizes now **rivals** desktop computers.

page 2

What to look for in a new laptop

✦ Look for this logo:

It means that the laptop is energy efficient: it consumes less energy and is environmentally friendly.

✦ To limit electronic waste, look for a laptop with a powerful processor, strong enough for the new technology that becomes available every year. It will last a long time and be a good investment.

✦ Make sure the laptop you want has a lot of USB ports. That way you can easily add on extras like a printer, a keyboard, a mouse, a storage unit, a **surround-sound system**, a multimedia projector, etc.

✦ If you're a **gamer** or are really into video, you will need a powerful video card.

page 3

My laptop computer checklist

✦ Before you buy your laptop, use this checklist to help you focus on what you need.

My laptop will replace my desktop computer. ☐

I need a light laptop because I will be carrying it a lot. ☐

I like a:

    small screen (30–36 cm) ☐

    average size (37–43 cm) ☐

    huge screen (over 43 cm) ☐

I want a good sound system. ☐

I need a CD/DVD player. ☐

I want a powerful battery. ☐

I want an extended warranty. ☐

My budget is _____.

page 4

Then

- With a partner, analyze this brochure. Complete the chart on your activity sheet.
- Make an overall evaluation of the brochure.

Finally

- Share your analysis and evaluation of the brochure with another pair of students.
- Be prepared to explain your evaluation.

Word Wise

This brochure is ... The slogan is ...	The text is ... The pictures are ...
very well done	dynamic
well chosen	powerful
easy to understand	hard to understand
not attractive	not clear
not catchy	confusing

Glossary

rugged = strong, robust
trekking = travelling on foot over difficult terrain
endorsement = paid recommendation
knowledgeable = well informed
expect = think, believe (of a future event)

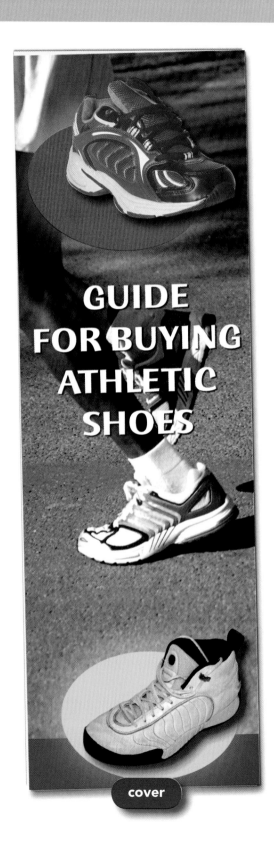

GUIDE FOR BUYING ATHLETIC SHOES

cover

THE RIGHT **SHOE** FOR **YOU**

There are many kinds of athletic shoes. There are shoes for walking, running, training or a combination of these activities. There are **rugged** athletic shoes for hiking and off-road **trekking**. Some are designed for specific sports like basketball or baseball.

So, first, you have to decide how you are going to use these shoes.

Then, you should find out what type of feet you have. Wet your feet and step on a dark surface. Look at your footprints to identify your foot type.

 ← Normal foot

 ← Flat foot

 ← High-arched foot

Tell the salesperson what type of feet you have.

page 2

What to look for in athletic shoes

Check for solid construction: well-sewn seams and no defects.

•

Buy quality. Select the best shoes within your budget so that they will last.

•

Keep in mind that some shoes are expensive because of the brand name, an athlete's **endorsement**, or their fashionable style.

•

Go to a store that has **knowledgeable** sales personnel. Ask lots of questions.

•

Try on shoes when your feet are swollen (after a workout or at the end of the day).

•

Wear the type of socks you will be wearing when you use your shoes.

•

Try on both shoes. Walk around the store. If possible, run or climb stairs.

•

Your shoes should be comfortable when you put them on. Don't **expect** the shoes to become more comfortable later on.

•

Make sure that your shoes are wide enough. You should be able to move your toes a bit.

page 3

If the shoe fits, wear it!

page 4

Producing a Brochure

❶ PREPRODUCTION

● Plan your project.

- With your team, choose your target audience for your "green" shopping guide: tweens, teens or adults.
- Make a list of things that this group likes to buy. Use the Internet or the library to do research on their consumer habits.
- Analyze this list. Are some of these items causing environmental issues? ••••••
- Look through Units 4 and 5 for ideas.
- Make a list of environmentally friendly consumer goods that the group could buy.
- Make a list of the environmentally damaging consumer goods to avoid.
- Search the Internet for design ideas and illustrations for your brochure.
- Refer to page 63 for the characteristics of effective brochures.
- Decide on the "green" message that you want to get across.
- Decide on the number of pages and on the content of each page.
- Decide which tasks each member of your team will do (research, pictures, text, layout, revision, etc.).

ENVIRONMENTAL ISSUES
• global warming and greenhouse effect
• hole in the ozone layer
• deforestation
• endangered animal species
• fossil fuels
• land pollution (waste)
• water pollution
• air pollution

❷ PRODUCTION

● Prepare a first draft.

- Write the first draft, using the brochures in this unit as models.
- Choose effective vocabulary. Write short, accurate sentences in order to send a clear message to your audience.
- Try different arrangements for your texts and pictures. Choose colours and fonts.
- Show your draft to another team of students. Use their feedback to make adjustments.

Media Alert

To get your message across, use slogans like *Think Green, Buy Smart.* A picture is worth a thousand words and so are logos. Use a logo that your audience will connect with.

- **Make the final version of your brochure.**
  - Create the brochure, taking the feedback from your classmates into account.
  - Revise and edit your texts carefully.
  - Make sure that your "green" message is easy to understand.
  - If computers are available, use software to produce a professional-looking product.
  - Ask yourself: Will this brochure make the audience take this issue seriously?

> **STRATEGY**
>
> Which strategies will help you check your work? See pages 205–207 in the Reference section.

❸ **POSTPRODUCTION**
- **Present your brochure to the class.**
  - Share the tasks of doing the presentation.
  - Name your intended audience and say how you plan to reach it. See the suggestions for reaching a wider audience.
  - State why you chose the topic for your presentation.
  - Get feedback on your brochure. Solicit reactions from the class about the issue and the products in your brochure.
- **Reflect on the project.**
  - Think back about what you learned in this unit and about the production process you used for this project.

WOrd Wise

What do you think of our brochure?
What suggestions can you make for improving it?
What is our brochure's message?
Do you agree or disagree with it?

REACHING A WIDER AUDIENCE

For tweens: Present the brochure to younger brothers or sisters, or to other tweens in your life.

For teens: Present the brochure to another class or to other teens in your life.

For adults: Present the brochure to your parents or to other adults in your life.

UNIT 7 That Was Then, This Is Now

◉ ASK YOURSELF ...

What do you know about dating and marriage through the ages? What are the different reasons couples got together in the past? Did they have romantic relationships? What about now? What are dating and marriage like today? Write down your ideas and opinions on your Action Plan sheet. ———————○

- Look at the pictures on pages 70 and 71 and read the descriptions.
- Which custom seems the strangest to you?
- Do you know of any other strange customs that we have today?
- What traditional gifts or symbols do people use to show their love today?
- Share your thoughts with the class.

Glossary

suitor = a man who wants to marry a particular woman
bundling = the custom of sleeping fully clothed with a fiancé
courting = interested in marrying one another
bride = woman on her wedding day
spouse = husband or wife

Strange Ways of Love

What was dating like in different times and places?

In England, if a gentleman of the late 1800s wanted to marry a woman, he sent her a pair of gloves. If the woman wore the gloves to church on Sunday, it meant that she accepted his offer of marriage.

FYI

It was in Scotland that women were first legally allowed to ask a man to marry them ... in 1228. This practice then slowly became legal across Europe.

As late as the 19th century, young men from some Native American tribes chose their mates during the Crane Dance. After getting the girl's mother's permission, the **suitor** came to the lodge while everyone was sleeping. He woke the girl, holding a light up to his face. If she blew out the light, he could stay and become part of her family.

"**Bundling**" came to North America with German settlers to Pennsylvania during the 17th century. It was an approved way for **courting** couples to visit one another—in bed! Houses were cold and roads were bad. Spending the night together fully clothed and wrapped tightly in blankets, with a board between them, made sense.

In 18th century Europe, when a **bride** left the church, a small loaf of bread was broken over her head. Unmarried guests picked up the pieces and placed them under their pillows. It was believed that this would help them dream of their future **spouse**.

In Wales in the 17th century, it was the custom for a man courting a woman to give her a "lovespoon." The carvings on this spoon meant "Marry me."

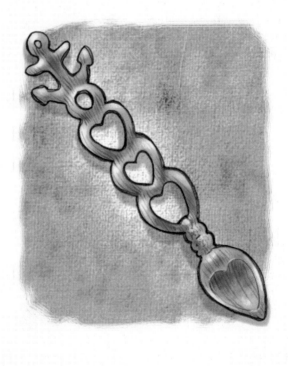

First

- Think about love and dating throughout the ages. In the past, whom do you think decided if a couple got married? Write your answer in your notebook.
- Before you read the text on page 73, look through it for unfamiliar words. Use the glossary and context cues to understand their meaning.

STRATEGY

Infer.
Look for context cues from the words before or after new words.

Next

- Read the text and check to see if your answer was correct.
- Look at the timeline. Reread the text and fill in the missing information on your activity sheet.
- Compare your answers with a partner.

Then

- What criteria do you think parents used for choosing a life partner for their child? Look at the text and write down two or three ideas.
- What criteria do you have for choosing a boyfriend or girlfriend?
- Share your ideas with a partner.

Finally

- Compare dating and marriage in the past with dating and marriage today. What are the main differences? Talk it over with your classmates.

WOrd Wise

In early civilizations, people ...
In the 17th century, they ...
On the other hand, today we ...
Now we ...
We don't have to ...

True Love?

Believe it or not, marrying for love is a concept that became popular only at the end of the 19th century.

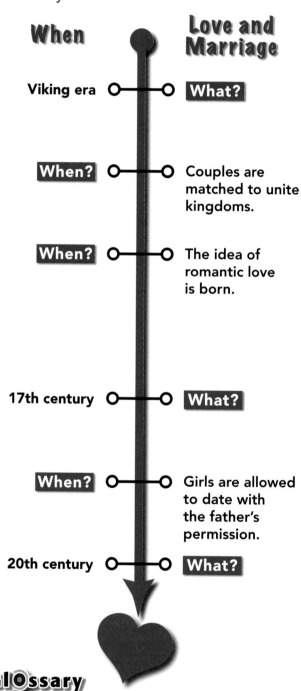

When — **Love and Marriage**

- Viking era — **What?**
- **When?** — Couples are matched to unite kingdoms.
- **When?** — The idea of romantic love is born.
- 17th century — **What?**
- **When?** — Girls are allowed to date with the father's permission.
- 20th century — **What?**

GlOssary

matchmaking = process of creating couples
well-suited = compatible
kingdoms = communities ruled by kings or queens
courtly = formal

Throughout history, there was little place for love in marriage **matchmaking**. Marriages were arranged by parents and families as an economic agreement. Marrying for love was considered ridiculous. People believed that love would not last. This is why parents, people of experience, chose their child's partner. This way, they could be sure that the couple was at least socially **well-suited**.

Keeping the peace

In early civilizations, the rules of love were determined by necessity. For example, when there were not enough young women in a Viking village, the men raided other villages for wives. During the Middle Ages, parents from the noble classes matched couples to solidify alliances and bring **kingdoms** together. Royals had to submit to matchmaking as a way of keeping the peace between nations. Couples often met for the first time on their wedding day.

Romantic love

In the 12th century, noblewomen in the royal courts of France became the objects of **courtly** love. During this period, strict rules of conduct were established for lovers. Although these rules were only for the aristocracy, it was the beginning of a more romantic era. This idea of romantic love slowly became accepted as the centuries progressed.

Daddy dearest

In the late 17th century, love was still not considered necessary before marriage. It was hoped that couples would learn to love each other after the wedding. During the Victorian era, men were allowed to call on young women of the upper classes only with the father's permission. During the meeting, the couple was rarely left alone. A chaperone was always around. Marriage proposals were often written and a woman could marry only if her father gave his consent.

Dating time

In the late 19th and early 20th centuries, dating was introduced. Increasingly, young people began to socialize together without adult supervision. By the mid-20th century, most young men and women had begun to trust their feelings rather than matchmakers. Finally, marrying for love was acceptable, even desired.

VOCABULARY

First

- Do you know how your parents or your grandparents met? Share what you know with your classmates.

Next

- Work with a partner. Decide who will read the interview with Charlotte on page 75 and who will read the interview with Richard on page 76.

- Read your text and then answer these questions by filling out the chart on your activity sheet together. ⋯⋯⋯⋯

Finally

- Is dating someone today so different from dating in the 1950s? Talk about your ideas with your classmates.

- Charlotte's and Richard's views of their future together are slightly different. Do you think this is typical of couples even today?

He Said ... She Said

In the 1950s, young men and women started dating freely. They relied on their feelings to find a partner.

	Charlotte said ...	Rich...said
1. Why did Charlotte and Richard not talk at the basketball game?	It was not appropriate ...	
2. What incident got them talking in the cafeteria?		
3. Why did Richard not kiss Charlotte on their first date?		

Glossary

scratch = make marks or cuts
dreamy = wonderful, like a dream

1956 Seaview High School Yearbook (SHSY)
Our Couple of the Year

We asked you to vote for the couple you feel is the most likely to get married. Your answers are in! We interviewed our two sweethearts, Charlotte and Richard. Read on to see how these two lovebirds met and how they see their future.

SHSY: Hi, Charlotte. So, tell us, what happened when you first met Richard?

Charlotte: Well, I first saw Richard at a school basketball game. I liked the way he smiled
5 and he had a nice laugh. But I didn't talk to him, not in front of everybody. That wouldn't have been appropriate.

SHSY: When did you two finally talk?

Charlotte: Well, I saw him at the school cafeteria.
10 He was standing behind me in the line. I intentionally dropped my fork and he picked it up. That's how we first started talking. We really hit it off. Unbelievably, he asked me out on a date. I was so happy!

SHSY: 15 What was your first date like?

Charlotte: **Dreamy.** Richard invited me to the Saturday sock hop. He came to my house to pick me up. We danced to Elvis's song "Love Me Tender." It was so romantic. He didn't
20 kiss me on our first date, but I could tell he wanted to. I'm glad he respected me enough to wait. Of course, now that we've been dating for so long, we kiss all the time (laughs).

SHSY: 25 Is your relationship strong? Will you stay together?

Charlotte: Absolutely. I think Richard and I will be together forever. He's so romantic and I know he will always take care of me.

FYI

When Elvis went on the Ed Sullivan TV show in 1957, they filmed him from the waist up. His pelvic movements were considered too provocative for TV!

SHSY: 30 Hi, Richard. So tell us what happened when you first met Charlotte?

Richard: Actually, it was pretty strange. I saw her at one of our basketball games. She looked really cute and I wanted to ask her out. Unfortunately, I had just 35 broken up with a girl and I was a little uneasy about asking Charlotte out. What if she didn't like me? I didn't want to look stupid in front of my friends.

SHSY: When did you two finally talk?

Richard: 40 Well, one day I was behind her in the cafeteria line. I gently bumped her tray so something would drop. Luckily, she dropped her fork and I picked it up. That gave me an excuse to talk to her. She was fun to talk with, so I asked her to 45 the sock hop. She said yes.

SHSY: What was your first date like?

Richard: I thought it was great. I picked her up in my dad's car. She looked so cute. I think I fell in love with her at the dance. I wanted to kiss her on that very first date but I was too nervous. Luckily, I'm 50 not nervous any more (laughs)!

SHSY: Is your relationship still strong? Will you stay together?

Richard: I believe so. I think Charlotte will be a good wife and she's great with children. 55 I'll go to college first and then, who knows? Maybe marriage.

SHSY: Well, there you have it everyone. Our lovebirds see a very long future together. We wish them lots of happiness. 60 They truly are lucky in love.

VOCABULARY

What's in a W⊙rd?

In English, many verbs are paired with a preposition that changes the meaning of the verb.

Examples:

to break = to destroy or to fall apart

to break up = to end a relationship

to ask = to pose a question or make a request

to ask (someone) out = to invite someone on a date

⊙ ASK YOURSELF...

What do you think now?

Look at the notes you wrote on your Action Plan sheet at the beginning of the unit. Is there anything you would like to add? Do you have any new ideas? Write them down in part 2. ————————○

Meet Your Mate

First

- Through the ages, history and literature have given us some unforgettable couples.
  - These famous couples are all mixed up. Match up the right partners. ••••••••••••••••→
  - What do you know about these couples? Share what you know with your classmates.

Then

- In these modern times, young couples talk about LUV via the Internet. It's a whole new language.
  - Look at the language used in chat rooms.
  - Try to decode the two messages. Write an answer to each in your notebook. Use the chat glossary as a guide.

Adam & Marge

Romeo & Josephine

Lancelot & Juliet

Antony & Eve

Homer & Cleopatra

Napoleon & Guinevere

---

hi2u
wnwu? im :-l. my g/f
is studyng. wanna
go to da gme l8r?
syl
marco

---

s^
i ws :-o u ddnt call
whr did u go ystrdy?
i mssd u. 143
wrud dis w-end?
my prnts say u cn
com for sppr
plz wbs
h&k, Julie

Chat Glossary

For starters

HI2U	→	hi to you
S^	→	What's up?

Emotions

:-o	→	surprised
:-|	→	bored
>:-(	→	angry
LOL	→	laugh out loud

Questions

WRUD	→	what are you doing?
WNWU	→	what's new with you?
whoz	→	who is
wanna	→	do you want to

Words of love

143	→	I love you
ILU2	→	I love you, too
B/F	→	boyfriend
G/F	→	girlfriend

Miscellaneous

IDN	→	I don't know
PLZ	→	please
WBS	→	write back soon
L8R	→	later

The alphabet

B → be		C → see	
R → are		U → you	
D → th (da → the; dat → that)			

Numbers

2 → to, too	
4 → for	
8 → "ate" sound	

Saying goodbye

SYL	→	see you later
H&K	→	hugs and kisses
TAFN	→	that's all for now
B4N	→	bye for now

Remember: When you chat, drop vowels from your words: ts fstr (it's faster).

Take shortcuts: Use abbreviations, numbers and symbols. Start a new line instead of using punctuation.

Asking Questions

1 **Show what you know.**

- Kareem is interviewing his grandmother. He has mixed up his notes. Help him out and match the answers to the questions.

  Questions
  a) Did you have a boyfriend when you were 15?
  b) When did you get married?
  c) What does your husband do?
  d) How many children do you have?
  e) Will you have more grandchildren?

  Answers
  1) Four.
  2) I hope so. My children are still young.
  3) No, I didn't. I started dating at 17.
  4) He is a retired teacher.
  5) I was 18.

- What do you notice about the verbs in the questions? What tenses are they?

2 **Review questions in the simple present tense.**

- To ask a question in the simple present tense,* use the auxiliary **do** (or **does** for the third-person singular) and the base form of the verb. Follow this word order:

Question Word (QW)	*do or does*	Subject	Verb	The rest of the sentence
	Do	you	want	to go out with me?
	Does	she	like	him?
What	do	you	do	for fun?
Where	does	Matty	live?	

3 **Practise.**

- Unscramble the questions.
  1. you / with Josh? / how often / go out / do
  2. Lauren? /does / why / Sam / like

4 **Review questions in the simple past tense.**

- To ask a question in the simple past tense,* use the auxiliary **did** and the base form of the verb. Follow this word order:

QW	*do or does*	Subject	Verb	The rest of the sentence
	Did	you	go	out with him?
When	did	they	meet?	

5 **Practise.**

- Unscramble the questions. Go back to pages 75 and 76 to find the answers.
  1. on the first date? / did / Charlotte / Richard / kiss
  2. talk / where / they / did / for the first time?

* The verb *to be* is an exception. See the chart on page 79.

6 Review questions in the future.

- To ask a question about the immediate future or to ask someone to do something, use the auxiliary **will** and the base form of the verb. Follow this word order:

QW	*will*	Subject	Verb	The rest of the sentence
When	will	Terry	ask	Delia to the prom?
	Will	you	mail	this letter for me?

- To ask a question about a future intention, we normally use the simple present of the verb **to be** + **going to** and the base form of the verb. Follow this word order:

QW	*to be*	Subject	*going to*	Verb	The rest of the sentence
	Are	you	going to	get	married?
Where	is	Caitlin	going to	buy	her prom dress?

For more on question words, go to page 194.

7 Practise.

- Unscramble the questions. Go back to pages 75 and 76 to find the answers.
  1. stay together? / will / Charlotte and Richard
  2. Richard / is / after high school? / going to / what / do

8 Now review questions with the verb *to be*.

- To ask a question in the simple present tense with the verb **to be**, follow this word order:

QW	*to be*	Subject	The rest of the sentence
	Is	your relationship	still strong?
Where	is	the dance?	

- To ask a question in the simple past tense with the verb **to be**, follow the same word order:

QW	*to be*	Subject	The rest of the sentence
	Was	Charlotte	at the dance with Richard?
Who	was	with you	last night?

- To ask a question about the immediate future with the verb **to be**, use the auxiliary **will** and the base form of the verb. Follow this word order:

QW	*will*	Subject	*to be*	The rest of the sentence
	Will	he	be	at your party?
When	will	they	be	here?

9 Practise.

You have set your best friend up on a **blind date**. Help him or her prepare some questions to get to know the girl or guy better. Write two questions in the simple present, two questions in the simple past and two questions in the future.

Glossary

blind date = a date with someone you have never met before

LANGUAGE WORKS

Exchanging Greetings and Information

1 **Look at the following language models.**

Social conventions	Requests for information
Nice to see you again.	Who is with Kim?
What's new?	Why didn't you come with Sami?
How have you been?	When did you arrive?
How are you doing?	What do you think of the party?
	Where are Carla and Luc?

2 **Form teams.**

- Practise using the language models. Greet your teammates. Ask each other the questions in the box. Give logical answers to the questions.

3 **Listen to the conversation.** 🎧

- Listen to the conversation some students are having at a party. They are talking about their evening.
- Pay attention to the different social conventions the students use to greet each other.
- Write down some examples as you listen.
- Listen again. This time, pay attention to how the students request information.

4 **Do a role play.**

- Your teacher will give you role-play cards. Read the information on your card.
- Imagine that you are at a school dance. Use social conventions to mix with the other people at the dance. Answer their questions based on the information on your role-play card.
- Ask others questions about what they see and hear around them. React to their comments to keep the conversation going.
- Listen carefully to what they say. You will need the information you hear later on.
- When you are finished, go back to your teams. Your teacher will direct this part of the activity.

STRATEGY

Remember you can use strategies to aid communication. See pages 205–207 for a complete list of strategies.

SELF-CHECK

☑ Think about the strategies you used. Which ones were most helpful to you? Which ones will you try to use the next time you interact orally?

Write On

◎ YOUR TASK

Write up an interview with your parents or your grandparents, or a couple you know who are dating.

Your text will contain:
- an opening statement that introduces the couple
- a separate paragraph for each question in the past, present and future
- a conclusion that summarizes your thoughts about the couple

❶ Plan your writing.

- Look at the models on pages 75 and 76.
- Look at your Action Plan notes and the texts in the unit for ideas for your questions.
- Write a list of questions about the couple's relationship. Make sure you include questions in the simple past, simple present and future.
- Interview the couple you have chosen. Note down their answers.
- Use an outline to help you organize your introduction, questions and answers, and conclusion. ••••••••••••••••••••••••••••

❷ Write a first draft of your text.

- Look at your outline to help you write up your interview.
- Use new words from your vocabulary log in your introduction and conclusion if you can.

❸ Revise and edit your text.

- Add, substitute, delete and rearrange ideas and words in your introduction and conclusion. Make sure the questions and answers are accurate.
- Edit your text using your checklist and other resources as needed.
- Ask someone to check your work.
- Write your final copy.

❹ Go public.

- Share your text with the class.

MY OUTLINE

Short introduction

Meet Danielle and Bertrand, my parents! They are ... I interviewed them to find out about ...

Questions about the past

first meeting?
met at a bus stop during a rainstorm
first date?
went to a ...
feelings in the beginning?
liked each other ...

Questions about the present

their relationship now?
do a lot of things together ...
what they like to do together?
dance, cook, ...

Questions about the future

their hopes for the future?
lots of grandchildren ...
plans for the future?
keep on having fun ...

Conclusion

I think my parents ... They ...

UNIT 8

Yo, Ho, Ho!

A Pirate's World

◎ **ASK YOURSELF ...**

What do you know about pirates? Do you think a pirate's life in the old days was exciting and **romantic**, or criminal and immoral? What does modern-day piracy mean to you? Write down your ideas and opinions on your Action Plan sheet.

- Work with a partner.
- Look at the illustration. Can you identify the numbered items?
- Use vocabulary from the Word Wise list.
- Write your answers in your notebook.

WOrd Wise

I think that's ... Isn't this ...?	That's called a ... I know: it's ...
captain	Jolly Roger
coast	pirate ship
crew	sails
deck	sword
eye patch	treasure chest
first mate	treasure map
gold	wooden leg
helm	

GlOssary

romantic = idealistic, fantastic

Pirate Times

First

- Look at the cover page of *Pirate Times* magazine on page 85. Which articles seem interesting to you?

Then

- Look over the texts *The Golden Age of Piracy* and *Life at Sea* on pages 86 to 89.
- Decide as a class how you want to read the texts: in teams, with a partner or on your own.
- Use the reading logs to organize the information in the texts.
- Share your findings with a classmate.

After that

- Learn to speak like a pirate on page 90.
- Solve a puzzle on page 91.

Next

- Read about two pirates, Grace O'Malley and Edward Teach, on pages 92 and 93.
- You can work in teams, with a partner or on your own.
- Use the reading logs to better understand the texts.

Then

- As a class, read the letters in the Reader's Corner on pages 94 and 95. Your teacher will direct this activity.

Finally

- Use all the information you collected to complete a Response Journal about piracy.

STRATEGY

Use strategies to understand the texts. Choose from these:

- Plan – What resources do you need?
- Infer – What do the pictures and title tell you about the text?
- Skim – What is the general idea of this text?
- Scan – What specific information are you searching for as you read this text?
- Self-monitor – Do you understand the text?
- Self-evaluate – What did you learn?

Or use other strategies that work for you.

Word Wise

I would like to read …
Do you agree?
What would you like to read?
Which text did you read?
What is your text about?
I learned that …

PIRATE TIMES

Everything you ever wanted to know about pirates

This month's READER'S CORNER
Piracy Today—Are You Part of the Problem?

THE GOLDEN AGE OF PIRACY
(1650 – 1725)

Pirates have **roamed** the seas for as long as there have been ships and sailors. However, during one **infamous** period, many dangerous pirates sailed the seas of the New World in search of
5 fame and fortune. Pirates like Captain Morgan, Captain Kidd and Blackbeard were both feared and admired. They were the anti-heroes of this era, known as the golden age of piracy. ●

Movies, novels and television greatly influence
10 what we know about pirates. Fictional works like *Treasure Island* and *Peter Pan* have become an important part of English culture. Despite the fact that pirates were criminals, Hollywood seems to like the idea of the heroic pirate. Just
15 think of Captain Jack Sparrow from the movie *Pirates of the Caribbean*. He is portrayed as a likeable bandit. In fact, many movies, such as *Captain Blood*, *The Pirates of Penzance* and *The Princess Bride*, show
20 pirates as romantic adventure heroes. ●

So, what makes us like pirate stories so much? Perhaps it is the notion
25 that pirates sailed the seas from adventure to adventure, getting rich in the process. That is the myth of piracy. But what are the facts?

Many pirates began their careers as honest
30 sailors. In the late 17th century, the warring nations of France, England and Spain signed peace treaties. Suddenly, sailors were **out of work**, so the chance to make money from **plunder** was very attractive. Many embarked
35 on a new career on the Caribbean Sea: piracy. Some historians believe that piracy was also an effective way to **climb the social ladder**. Pirate Captain Henry Morgan, for example, eventually became Deputy Governor of
40 Jamaica. ⬡

The seas of the New World

Captain Blood

Glossary
roamed = traveled around
infamous = famous for being bad
out of work = unemployed
plunder, booty = stolen goods, treasure
climb the social ladder = improve their
    position in society
marooned = abandoned on a deserted island

But the fact is that pirates were criminals: they made a living by stealing other people's property. Pirates were cruel and often barbaric. They knew their victims would surrender more easily if they were afraid. Those who resisted were **marooned** and their ships were burned.

Because a pirate's life was hard and cruel, it was considered a man's world. However, there were a few women pirates. Women like Mary Read and Anne Bonny became pirates by dressing like men. They had to show considerable strength and courage to survive. ●

Pirate ships were small, fast and powerful, so they could overtake most merchant ships. They could easily travel along the coast and hide in small, secluded bays.

Surprisingly, most pirate ships were run democratically. Pirates elected their captain and everyone obeyed his orders during battle.

But the crew made all the other decisions as a group, from where to sail to dividing the **booty**. They wrote a list of rules at the beginning of the voyage that everyone agreed to follow. ●

A democratic way of life, a beautiful setting and tales of adventure inspired by books and films have probably contributed to our romantic vision of the pirate captain and his courageous crew. ●

VOCABULARY

Pirate Mary Read

Pirates in pursuit of a merchant ship

FYI

References to pirates are found in Homer's *Iliad* and *Odyssey*, epic poems that date back to the 7th century BC!

Life at Sea

So you think life at sea was a wonderful adventure? In reality, the life of a pirate was neither easy nor romantic.

What's for dinner?

5 The food **aboard** pirate ships was terrible. Pirates spent months at sea, so the food often **went bad.** They mostly ate salted pork, biscuits and dried fruit. In port, they sometimes had chicken or meat. Pirates also ate fish and 10 turtles when other food was hard to find. Most of the time, they were hungry. They drank alcohol because the ship's drinking water did not stay fresh for very long.

All hands on deck!

15 Apart from **manning** the sails and taking part in battles, pirates had to do specific chores. Each pirate had a schedule to follow. Sometimes, they had to **scrub** the decks. At other times, they had to watch for other ships 20 and for signs of bad weather. Throughout the night, they took turns sailing the boat and keeping watch.

Who's who of a crew

The captain had to follow the rules like the rest 25 of the crew. His main role was commanding the pirates during battle. He also received a bit more of the stolen treasure. The quartermaster was the negotiator between the captain and the crew. He also kept a record of how much 30 treasure the crew had. The boatswain organized the distribution of food and drink. He set up schedules for cleaning the boat. The carpenter maintained and repaired the ship.

Glossary

aboard = on a ship
went bad = became rotten, tasted terrible
manning = operating
scrub = rub hard to clean, wash
who's who = the most important people

Fun and games

35 Music and singing were a very important part of pirate life. Pirates often forced captured musicians to remain on board to play for them. Pirates also played cards and rolled dice to pass the long hours, but they were not permitted to 40 **gamble**.

Is there a doctor on board?

Some pirate ships had surgeons on board but they were usually very incompetent. Carpenters often had to take on the role of surgeons. They 45 treated their patients with the same tools they used to fix the ship! Also, medicine was rare. Many pirates died from their battle injuries or from diseases caused by bad food, water and hygiene.

50 How much are you **worth**?

During battles, some pirates were badly injured. Sometimes they lost an eye or had to have a **limb** cut off. These pirates received extra gold from the booty. Pirates often decided 55 before the voyage how much each limb was worth. For example, some pirates decided that a leg was worth 600 pieces of gold and a hand was worth 300.

VOCABULARY

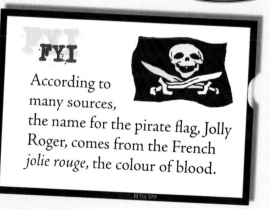

FYI

According to many sources, the name for the pirate flag, Jolly Roger, comes from the French *jolie rouge*, the colour of blood.

Glossary

gamble = bet money on a game
worth = valued
limb = arm or leg

PIRATE-SPEAK

You may have noticed that pirates in fiction and in movies speak their own brand of English. Here is a **crash course** in pirate-speak that should help you master the language.

Let's start with the basics.

You say	A pirate says
Hi! Hey! Oh, wow! I agree. I'll do it immediately, Mom!	Ahoy! Avast! Shiver me timbers! Aye! Aye, aye!

Now observe the word order for the following questions.

You say	A pirate says
Are you going …? What are you doing? Who are you waiting for? Where is …? Is that …?	Be ye goin' …? What be ye doin'? Who be ye waitin' for? Whar be …? Be that …?

Here are some words and expressions you may find useful.

boy = lad
the washroom = t' head
the mall = t' market
would like = be needin'
feel like = be hankerin'
to eat = t' stuff me boghole
the bank = t' buried treasure

girl = lass
the cafeteria = t' galley
my friend = me bucko
to drink = t' swill
go shopping = pillage 'n' plunder
beverage = grog
Pardon me, sir. = Avast, matey!

And if you don't know the proper word or expression, just throw in an **Arrr!** or two. It can mean just about anything, so it's the most useful word in pirate-speak.

Someone says	A pirate answers
I have a headache. Do you feel like playing computer games?	Arrr! Arrr! Arrr!

Now try your voice and change the following lines into pirate-speak.
1. Pardon me, sir. Where is the washroom?
2. The boys would like something to drink.
3. Hi, Katy. Are you going to the cafeteria?
4. My friend and I are going to the mall.
5. We feel like shopping.

Shiver me timbers!

Glossary
crash course = short lesson

CAPTAIN JIM'S TREASURE MAP

According to legend, pirates often drew puzzling maps to make sure that other pirates did not steal their treasure. If you can decode this treasure map, you will discover what Captain Jim buried.

- Using the clues on this page, find the towns on the map you need to visit to solve the puzzle. Visit each town only once.
- Write the letter indicated at the end of each clue into your notebook.
  Example: 1. *Start at a town that is almost an island* = Presque Isle, so the fourth letter = S.

1. Start at a town that is almost an island. (fourth letter)
2. Go north to the town where the large reindeer roam. (fourth letter)
3. Quick, go south to see the president. (first letter)
4. Head southwest to the town that is never thirsty. (sixth letter)
5. Continue your travels northeast to the sea, just west of Canada. (first letter)
6. Now go southwest to the town of liberty. (second letter)
7. Take a short trip to clean up your act. (second letter)
8. Now travel further west to meet the red-haired lady. (sixth letter)
9. Go northeast to see the man who grows flowers. (fourth letter)
10. Move north in the eighth month of the year. (third letter)
11. Continue northeast to a town filled with noise. (fifth letter)
12. Go back south to a rocky harbour. (fifth letter)
13. Finally, travel southwest to where the ships come in from the sea. (eighth letter)

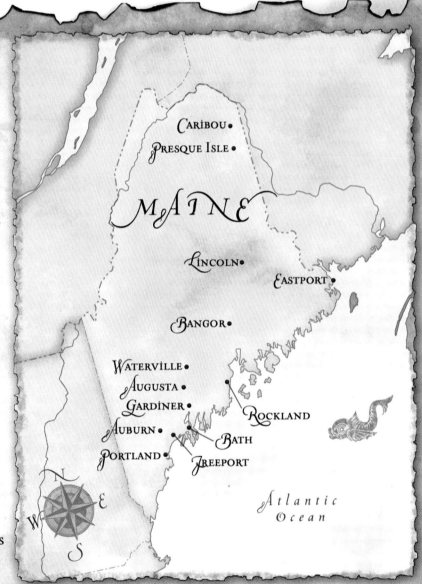

Captain Jim's treasure is ...

S	?	?	?	?	?	?	?	?	?	?	?	?
1	2	3	4	5	6	7	8	9	10	11	12	13

Word Wise

What do you think the answer is?
What do you suggest for this one?
I think it might be ... What's your opinion?
That's it! Good thinking!

And now for the continuing story of Ireland's most famous pirate queen

The Adventures of
Grace O'Malley, Pirate Queen
(Part 3)

The pirate crew was restless as they approached the ship. They were waiting for a signal from their leader. "Attack! Attack!" Captain Grace O'Malley finally shouted. The
5 pirates, led by O'Malley, jumped on board the Spanish ship and quickly took control. "Take the gold and set the men free," she ordered. "Without their ship and arms, they are harmless." Her crew released the Spanish sailors. They
10 escaped to shore in a small boat. ●

Grace O'Malley looked proudly at her men. "You fought well. Now let's divide the treasure!" The men cheered and started to line up. As she was distributing the gold, the pirates were
15 discussing the battle. "T' was a fierce fight," said Slim Jim. "While I was struggling with one sailor, two others jumped on me! I was lucky ye were there t' save me, Brawny," the young pirate thanked his friend.

20 "Aye, bucko," replied the big, muscular pirate. "That be teamwork!" It was true, Slim Jim thought. The pirates here on the west coast of Ireland worked well together. Life under the leadership of Grace O'Malley, the Pirate Queen, was certainly
25 exciting. They had captured many ships and the gold had been plentiful. "Aye," Jim agreed. ●

Later that night, as O'Malley was standing at the helm, a sense of **uneasiness** came over her. "Thar' be a change in the wind, Captain,"
30 whispered No-Neck Rico, the first mate. "I feel it too, Rico. Ready the crew."

The cold, fierce storm came up very fast. The rain came down hard and the wind was fearful. The captain and crew had never experienced
35 such a storm before.

The waves tossed the ship around like a toy. Grace O'Malley desperately held on to the ship's helm. She knew the fate of her crew was in her hands. She had to sail her ship to safe harbour.
40 There was a loud crack. The foremast **came crashing down** toward the deck. The crew ran for cover. Then, in the **howling** wind she heard the cry "**Man overboard!**" It was Slim Jim. ●

(To be continued next month)

Glossary

uneasiness = worry, anxiety
came crashing down = fell down with a loud
   noise
howling = sounding like the cry of a wolf
man overboard = someone fell off the boat

FYI

Grace O'Malley was a real pirate captain who roamed the seas off the west coast of Ireland in the late 16th century. She started sailing at a young age, married twice, went to prison twice, and commanded a crew of over 200 pirates.

Featured Pirate of the Month

CAPTAIN EDWARD "BLACKBEARD" TEACH

The most notorious captain of the golden age of piracy was, without a doubt, Captain Edward "Blackbeard" Teach.

According to legend, Edward Teach was a cruel
5 and heartless pirate. He was a big man with a formidable weapon—the ability to **strike fear** in people, including his crew. A great black beard covered most of his face, **hence** the name Blackbeard. Before battle, Blackbeard **braided**
10 his beard and put gunpowder and slow-burning fuses in the braids. He lit the fuses, causing smoke to surround his face. With his flaming red coat, two swords at his waist, pistols and **daggers**, he was both spectacular and terrifying. But
15 Blackbeard rarely engaged in battle. The sight of him was enough to make most of his victims surrender immediately. ◉

Blackbeard allowed those who surrendered to sail away—after he had taken their weapons,
20 booty and rum, of course! Those who resisted were marooned and their ship set on fire. Blackbeard certainly looked like a demon, but some historians claim he never actually killed anyone until the battle that led to his own
25 death. ◉

Blackbeard began his pirate career in 1713 as a crewman on board a ship commanded by the pirate Benjamin Hornigold. The two men spread fear throughout the Caribbean. In 1717
30 Hornigold retired from piracy, but Blackbeard continued his reign of terror. He commanded four vessels and a crew of over 300 pirates.

In 1718 Blackbeard **met his fate** near Ocracoke Island, off the coast of North Carolina. His
35 career as a pirate lasted only a few years. But in that time, Blackbeard captured over 40 ships and plundered his way to notoriety. ◉

Glossary
strike fear = inspire fear
hence = for this reason
braided = twisted three
  strands of hair together
daggers = small, pointed
  knives
met his fate = died (in battle)
  as expected

What's in a Word?
VOCABULARY

RESTLESS   HARMLESS   HEARTLESS

These words all end with the suffix –less, which means "without."
• Can you guess their meaning?
• What about the words PLENTIFUL and FEARFUL?
• Do you know any other words with these endings?

Piracy Today—Are You Part of the Problem?

In last month's issue we dealt with modern-day piracy (illegal downloading of music and films, plagiarism, etc.). The subject seemed to **touch a sore spot** with many of you. A lot of people responded. Here are some of our readers' opinions. Tell us what you think.

To the editor of *Pirate Times*,

It's **high time** people realized that piracy does not just happen on the high seas. These days, people constantly commit acts of piracy when they copy material that does not legally belong to them. They download computer games onto their computers, share MP3s or burn CDs for their friends. In other words, just like pirates, they are stealing. This might seem harmless, but it is illegal and, in my opinion, wrong. ●

Music sales are falling because so many people are downloading music and copying CDs. Studies show that 21% of the population (12 to 24 year olds) are responsible for almost 80% of all online theft in Canada. Some claim they plan to buy the CD later. However one quarter of this group admit that they never bought the album or song they downloaded. Their excuse: artists are already rich and don't need the money. ●

I say that it is not right to steal these products. Artists put all their creative energy into making them. They invest time and money and deserve to **reap** the rewards. If downloading and illegal burning continue, jobs will be lost. In the end, we all pay a price for this. Software piracy and illegal copying of material is costing the economy millions. ●

Paul Sauvé,
Longueuil, QC

Gl●ssary

touch a sore spot = get a strong response
high time = urgent
reap = receive, collect
bootlegging = recording illegally
fined = forced to pay money for doing
    something illegal

To the editor of *Pirate Times*,

I admit it: I am a pirate. I occasionally copy some homework from a friend at school. But what choice do I have? If I don't copy, I won't get all my homework done on time. At school the pressure is on to get good results. That means I sometimes have to cheat a little to hand in good papers. I don't think it is right but I really don't have the time to finish all my assignments. ●

Don't complain about modern-day piracy. Be honest. Who hasn't copied a math answer, or cut-and-pasted in an essay without naming the source? Who else am I really hurting? If anyone is hurt, it will be me. It's my education. ●

Anthony Garneau
Gaspé, QC

To the editor,

I am in a state of shock. At the movie theatre last Saturday, I saw a sign at the door warning against video recording during the show. I can't believe that people are actually **bootlegging** movies in the movie theatre. What are these people thinking? If they record movies illegally, well, the price of a movie ticket will probably double or triple! If this continues, managers of theaters might ask that we leave our bags at the front desk. We might even be searched as we walk through the door—what a violation of our rights! ●

I love going to the movies and I am angry that some people are breaking the rules. All because they want to make a few extra dollars recording a movie that honest people are paying to watch. I think these pirates should be **fined** hundreds of dollars. And, if they don't stop, the police should throw them in jail! ●

Andréanne Charbonneau
Beauport, QC

DUE TO PIRACY ISSUES WE ASK
THAT YOU PLEASE PLACE YOUR BAG ON
THE FLOOR AND NOT ON THE SEAT
NEXT TO YOU

THANK YOU

◎ **ASK YOURSELF...**
What do you think now?

Look at the notes you wrote on your Action Plan sheet. Have you changed your mind about anything? Do you have any new ideas about modern-day piracy? Write them down in part 2. ———●

Reaching a Consensus

1 Look at the following language models.

Opinions and clarification	Agreement and disagreement
What's your opinion?	Do we all agree?
How do you feel about it?	We all agree that …
I'm not sure.	We don't agree on Article …
What do you mean?	Why not?

2 Form teams.

- Brainstorm for other language you already know for exchanging opinions, asking for clarification, and agreeing and disagreeing.

> **STRATEGY**
> Remember you can use strategies to aid communication. See pages 205–207 for a complete list of strategies.

3 Listen to the conversation. 🎧

- These students are having a conversation about their school's code of conduct.
- Pay attention to the language they use as they exchange opinions, ask for clarification, and agree or disagree.
- Write down a few examples as you listen. Share them with your teammates.
- Listen to the recording again and note what parts of the code Suzy and Marc agree with. What do they disagree with?

4 Read the pirate code of conduct.

- On your own, choose five articles that, in your opinion, are the most important on a pirate ship.
- Discuss your choices with your team and come to a consensus on the five most important articles.
- Be ready to defend your opinion.
- Remember, your whole team must agree on the same five essential articles.

Before they set out to sea, pirates met on their ship and wrote a code of conduct. This code described how the pirates should act and the consequences if they did not follow the rules.

CODE OF CONDUCT

ARTICLE 1

Every pirate will have one share of the treasure. The captain will receive one share and a half. The quartermaster, carpenter and boatswain will have one share and a quarter.

ARTICLE 2

The captain will decide where the ship will sail and which ships to attack.

ARTICLE 3

If a pirate steals from another pirate or steals more than his portion of the plunder, he will be marooned.

ARTICLE 4

A pirate who strikes another pirate will receive 40 lashes of the whip.

ARTICLE 5

The musicians will rest one day of the week.

ARTICLE 6

If a pirate tries to run away, he will be marooned.

ARTICLE 7

A pirate who loses a limb in battle will receive extra shares of the treasure.

ARTICLE 8

A pirate who does not clean his weapons will receive 40 lashes of the whip.

ARTICLE 9

A pirate who uses an open flame on the ship and puts the ship in danger of fire will do double duties.

ARTICLE 10

Any pirate who shows cowardice during battle will be marooned.

FYI

Robinson Crusoe, a book by Daniel Defoe about a man who was marooned on a deserted island, was based on the true story of Alexander Selkirk.

SELF–CHECK

☑ Think about the strategies you used. Which ones were most helpful to you? Which ones will you try to use the next time you interact orally?

GRAMMAR WORKS

Expressing Real Conditions

1 **Show what you know.**

Sentences with *if* are called conditional sentences.
They are divided into two parts: the if-clause and the main clause.

- These pirates are using two types of conditional sentences to express real conditions. ••••••••••

- Which verbs are used in the if-clause? Which are used in the main clause?

If we follow this map, we will find the treasure.

We can find it before sundown if we sail quickly.

2 **Learn about if-clauses that express real conditions.**

- Real conditions describe what is possibly, probably or certainly going to happen as a result of something else. The if-clause contains the **condition** and the main cause contains the **result**.

  If a pirate steals from his crew, they will leave him on a desert island.
            condition   **result**

  Music sales will probably drop if people continue to download music illegally.
            result   **condition**

Affirmative Statements

- Notice that the if-clause (condition) is always in the present tense. The verb in the main (result) clause changes depending on the meaning you want to express.
  If you use illegal software on your computer,
  - ➡ you put yourself at risk.   (simple present = certainty)
  - ➡ your hard drive can be in danger.   (*can* + verb = possibility)
  - ➡ you will have problems with your programs.   (future simple = probability)
  - ➡ you could be in trouble.   (*could* + verb = possibility)
  - ➡ you might lose some of your files.   (*might* + verb = possibility)
  - ➡ you should replace it with legal software.   (*should* + verb = suggestion)

- The if-clause can be placed before or after the main clause. When it is before, we separate the two clauses with a comma.
  If you buy your CDs, the music industry will continue to do well.

- When the if-clause comes last, we do not use a comma.
  The price of movie tickets will continue to rise if people continue to buy bootleg DVDs.

Negative Statements

- The if-clause can contain a negative statement.
  If people **do not stop** copying movies,
    - ➥ the price of movie tickets **will rise**. (future simple = probability)
    - ➥ movie theatres **might disappear**. (*might* + verb = possibility)

  If you **do not want** music sales to drop,
    - ➥ you **should not** copy CDs. (*should* + verb = suggestion)
    - ➥ **do not** copy CDs. (imperative = strong suggestion)

Questions

- If-clauses can also be used to ask questions about real conditions.
  Will the music industry **survive** if people **continue** to burn CDs?
  What **happens** if a pirate **tries** to run away?
  Do pirates **get** a bigger share of the booty if they loose a limb during battle?

For more on if-clauses, go to page 197.

③ Practise.

   A. Go back and reread the three letters to the editor on pages 94 and 95.

- As you read, find six conditional sentences and write them in your notebook. Use a T-chart to list the verbs used in the if-clause and those in the main clause.

If-clause	Main clause

- Decide if these conditional sentences express a certainty, possibility, probability or suggestion.

   B. Match the if-clauses to the correct main clauses.

1. If you download computer software,
2. Authorities will consider you a criminal
3. Artists will demand more money for their CDs
4. If people become aware of the dangers of illegal copying,
5. If you rent a DVD,

a) if you record movies in the movie theatre.
b) a portion of the rental fee goes to the movie maker.
c) they will stop.
d) you could damage your computer.
e) if people continue to download their music illegally.

- Compare your answers with a partner. Together, reach an agreement on the right answer for each statement.

Write On

◎ YOUR TASK

Write a letter giving your opinion on piracy in the Golden Age or on modern-day piracy.

Your letter will contain:
- an introduction explaining the purpose of your letter
- a separate paragraph for each argument you have that supports your opinion
- a conclusion that summarizes your major points ⸺⚬

1 **Plan your writing.**
- Look at the texts on pages 94 and 95. Use the same structure for your text.
- Think about the things you learned in this unit about piracy.
- Look at your Action Plan notes and the texts in this unit for ideas.
- Decide on the subject of your letter. Choose from the following topics:
  - Pirates: romantic heroes or vicious criminals?
  - Downloading music, copying CDs: what's right, what's not?
  - Is bootlegging an act of piracy? What about copying DVDs?
  - Copying homework: it's OK, isn't it?
- Construct an outline of your letter. ⋯⋯⋯▸
- Look at the outline model on page 101 to help you structure your letter.

2 **Write a first draft of your text.**
- Follow your outline to make sure you include all your arguments to support your opinion.
- Use new words from your vocabulary log.

OUTLINE

Salutation

Opening paragraph
State the reason for writing the letter. Make your opinion clear.

Second paragraph
Give a strong argument supporting your opinion.

Third paragraph
Give another argument supporting your opinion.

Conclusion
Restate your opinion and main supporting arguments.

Signature
Sign your letter.

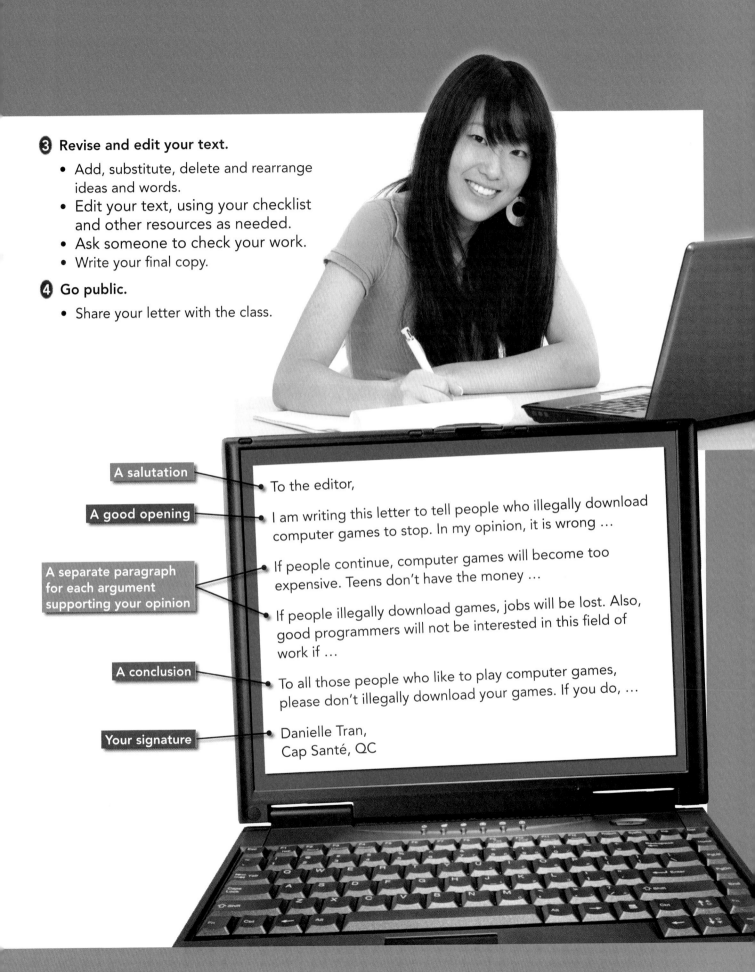

3 **Revise and edit your text.**

- Add, substitute, delete and rearrange ideas and words.
- Edit your text, using your checklist and other resources as needed.
- Ask someone to check your work.
- Write your final copy.

4 **Go public.**

- Share your letter with the class.

A salutation

To the editor,

A good opening

I am writing this letter to tell people who illegally download computer games to stop. In my opinion, it is wrong …

A separate paragraph for each argument supporting your opinion

If people continue, computer games will become too expensive. Teens don't have the money …

If people illegally download games, jobs will be lost. Also, good programmers will not be interested in this field of work if …

A conclusion

To all those people who like to play computer games, please don't illegally download your games. If you do, …

Your signature

Danielle Tran,
Cap Santé, QC

UNIT 9 Project: Newsletter Alert

Looking at Teen Issues

Your best friend is dating your ex-girlfriend or ex-boyfriend.

ANSWER THIS ...

In the past two units, you looked at rules of conduct like the respect of property and copyright. You have also seen how social behaviours, manners and etiquette have evolved over the years.

What advice can you offer for difficult situations or dilemmas that teens face?

With a classmate, talk about these issues.

- In your opinion, which of the situations shown on this page is the most difficult?
- Which ones are problematic for you?
- Do you have solutions to suggest?
- What other situations or dilemmas do teens have to face?

A friend is photocopying a new book.

A locker partner is always leaving old food and dirty gym clothes in your locker.

You introduce your date to your parents for the first time.

A friend is always borrowing money without paying it back.

Word Wise

That's a really difficult situation.
I had that experience.
Here is what I did.
I have a solution for that.
I guess you should say ...

A friend is always **gossiping** about you and everyone else.

Glossary

gossiping = talking about other people's private lives

YOUR PROJECT

Decide on two difficult situations or dilemmas that you want to address. Present the situations or dilemmas and your proposed solutions in an original and creative manner as part of a newsletter for teens.
Present your newsletter to the class.

- Think about these questions.
  1. Where do you usually see newsletters?
  2. What kinds of newsletters do you see?
  3. What characteristics do they have?
  4. What sort of messages do they contain?

- Here are some of the characteristics of a successful newsletter.

CHARACTERISTICS OF A SUCCESSFUL NEWSLETTER

An effective newsletter ...

- has an original style that is easily identifiable

- uses catchy titles to grab the reader's attention

- makes readers feel that they are part of a community

- asks readers to respond to the content

- speaks directly to its target audience in clear, simple language

- has visuals that complement the text and capture the reader's interest

- provides useful information on issues that are important to its readers

- organizes the texts and visuals for easy reading

Deconstructing a Newsletter

First

- Look carefully at the newsletter on pages 105, 106 and 107.
- Analyze the first page of the newsletter on page 105 and answer these questions.
  1. What grabs your attention first?
  2. What do you notice about the texts?
  3. Are the language and illustrations suitable for high-school students?
  4. Are the topics interesting for this audience?
  5. What do you think of the artwork and photos?
  6. Are the colours effective?
  7. Are the titles catchy?

Next

- With a partner, analyze the second and third pages of the newsletter on pages 106 and 107. Complete the chart on your activity sheet. ••••••••••••••••••
- Make an overall evaluation of the newsletter.
- Share your analysis and evaluation of the newsletter with another pair of students.

Finally

- Together, discuss the solutions proposed on the second and third pages of the newsletter. Are they effective?
- Be prepared to explain the reasons for your opinion.

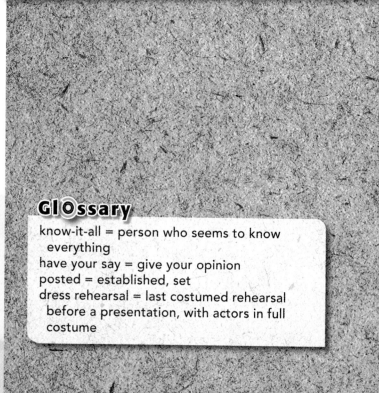

	Yes	N
Analysis of the newsletter		
1. Are the language and illustrations suitable for high-school students?		
2. Are the topics interesting for this audience?		
3. Are the visuals effective?		
4. Are the titles catchy?		
5. Is the text easy to understand?		
6. Are the problems realistic?		
7. Are the solutions helpful and practical?		
8. Is there anything that you don't like?		
Evaluation of the newsletter		
Content of the newsletter		
Presentation of the newsletter		

WOrd Wise

This newsletter is …
The pictures are …
The text is …
  (not) attractive
  (not) clear
  (not) easy to understand
  (not) funny
  (not) helpful
  (not) practical

GlOssary

know-it-all = person who seems to know everything
have your say = give your opinion
posted = established, set
dress rehearsal = last costumed rehearsal before a presentation, with actors in full costume

Cartier High Newsletter
from teens, for teens

Volume 2, Winter Issue

SPECIAL ISSUE
ADVICE FOR TEENS

Ms. Know-It-All
tells it like it is, and you **have your say**
on pages 2 and 3.

Another Win for Audrey

Audrey Lavallée **posted** a record time in the 100-metre sprint last weekend. She is going to the Québec Games again this summer. Congratulations, Audrey. Cartier High is very proud of you.

Get a sneak preview of
Romeo and Juliet

The Drama Club will be holding the **dress rehearsal** of their upcoming play, *Romeo and Juliet*, at noon on March 22 in the auditorium. The rehearsal is open to students and teachers only. Admission is one loonie.

  VOLLEYBALL GAME
Cartier High Cougars
vs.
Lennoxville Lions

March 14, 16:00
In school gym
Free admission

MEETINGS

- **Yearbook committee** meets every Wednesday at noon in Room 1672.
- **Year-end school activity committee** meets every Monday at 16:00 in Room 2032.

SCHOOL CAFETERIA
New menu starting this month

Friday vegetarian pizza special
99 cents for two slices

WOW !

HUMOUR

Be careful with punctuation.
Which version do you prefer?

Woman, without her man, is nothing.
Woman! Without her, man is nothing.

HOW TO DEAL WITH DIFFICULT SITUATIONS

In our last issue, we asked you to write in with problems or dilemmas that are troubling you. The response was enthusiastic. Here is this week's featured letter and the solution proposed by your favourite advisor, Ms. Know-It-All.

#1 NEW STUDENT BLUES

Dear Ms. Know-It-All,

Two weeks ago, a new student joined our class. Let's call him "Brad." He was **pretty shy** and he sat in the back of the class. He was very polite when anyone spoke to him, but most of the time, he was left alone. I was feeling kind of sorry for him. I was a new student last year, and no one talked to me for the first three weeks—what a terrible feeling!

A week ago, the Science teacher assigned a project. We were only three in our group, so I asked Brad to join us. He was very happy and he really worked hard on the project. But, here's my problem.

Brad follows me everywhere: to the cafeteria, to the library, to the bus stop. Sure, he's a nice guy, but I need my space. What can I do?

Freedom Lover

Dear Freedom Lover,

Well, first you have to talk to Brad about your feelings. Tell him you appreciate his work on the project, but that you need your own space. You may want to introduce him to other students who you think might accept him. Tell him about some of the school clubs. But make it clear that he can't follow you around all the time. Do keep an eye on him. He could turn out to be a good friend. Good luck.

Ms. Know-It-All

Last month, we described the dilemma faced by Dave. Some of you wrote in to offer Dave advice.

#2 PIRATED MUSIC FILES

Dave's dilemma

Dave lent some MP3 files of his uncle's rock group, the Agitators, to his friend Marc. Without permission, Marc made several copies and gave them away to students at school. Now Dave's uncle is upset with him.

Your advice

Hi Dave,

Your friend, is he really a friend? He should have asked for permission to make copies.

*Dave, my man, you got **burned**. It's so easy to copy these files that people forget there are copyrights.*

Hey, Dave.

*You'd better **blast** your "friend" Marc! If everybody keeps on pirating, musicians will stop producing original music!*

Dave's solution

Dave confronted Marc with the fact that he doesn't respect the property of others. He told Marc that he had no right to copy the files. He pointed out that his uncle makes his living and provides for his family with the money he makes from recordings and concerts. Dave and Marc are no longer friends.

Glossary

pretty shy = very shy
burned = tricked, cheated
blast = criticize strongly

Here's one issue that seems to be worrying a few of our readers. For reasons of confidentiality, we decided to summarize the situation in comic-strip format. Let's just call it ...

#3 DAD'S NEW GIRLFRIEND

Angie meets her father's new girlfriend.

Angie's dilemma

What can Angie say in this **touchy** situation? What can she do to get through this surprise meeting?

Ms. Know-It-All's solution

Angie can **take a few deep breaths**. She should try to be polite and not stress out. She has to speak to her father alone as soon as possible. She has to tell him that he should have told her about Courtney before he introduced her. Angie may have a hard time getting used to a new woman in her father's life—or maybe not. Her father seems to be happier than she has seen him in a long time. Maybe Courtney will make her visits to her father's apartment more fun. Plus, if Courtney can cook, at least the food will be better.

Glossary

touchy = delicate, uncomfortable
take a few deep breaths = try to relax

Producing a Newsletter

1 PREPRODUCTION

● **Plan your project.**

- With your team, choose two or more difficult situations or dilemmas that Secondary III students may encounter. ············▶
- Find solutions that can resolve them.
- Design a "How to Deal with Difficult Situations" newsletter. Use the second and third pages of the Cartier High newsletter on pages 106 and 107 as models.
- The situations can be presented in letter form or in an illustrated format (photo story, illustration, comic strip, etc.).
- Get ideas for content and language from Units 7 and 8.
- If computers are available, search the Internet for topics and newsletter designs.
- Refer to page 103 for the characteristics of a successful newsletter.
- Decide what tasks each member of your team will do (research, finding pictures, making illustrations, text, layout, revision, etc.).

2 PRODUCTION

● **Prepare a first draft.**

- Write the first draft, using appropriate language according to the format you have chosen: letter, comic strip, etc.
- Try different arrangements for your texts and pictures.
- Choose colours and fonts.
- Show your draft to another team of students. Use their feedback to make adjustments.

TEEN ISSUES

- A friend asks to copy your homework.
- A friend shoplifts while you are shopping together.
- A classmate dies in a car accident.
- A classmate tells you she is pregnant.
- You see a classmate cheating during an examination.
- Your mother or father wants you to meet his or her new partner.
- Other teen issues that you have encountered.

Media Alert
Capture your readers' interest with original ideas, catchy titles and a creative presentation.

What's in a WOrd?

- When writing the newsletter, use natural, everyday language. This will give your readers the impression that you are speaking to them directly.

- **Make the final version of your newsletter.**
  - Create the newsletter, taking the feedback from your classmates into account.
  - Revise and edit your texts carefully.
  - Make sure that the situations and solutions can be easily understood.
  - If computers are available, use software to produce a polished product.
  - Ask yourself: Will this newsletter make readers take these issues seriously?

3 POSTPRODUCTION
- **Present your newsletter to the class.**
  - Share the tasks of doing the presentation.

> **STRATEGY**
>
> Which strategies will help you with your presentation?
> See pages 205–207 in the Reference section.

  - To get your message across, role play or present in a dramatic fashion one of the dilemmas from your newsletter.
  - State why you chose the topic for your presentation.
  - Get feedback on your newsletter.
  - Solicit reactions from the class about the issue.

- **Reflect on the project.**
  - Think back about what you learned in this unit and about the production process you used.

WOrd Wise

What do you think of our dilemma and our solution?
What suggestions for improvement can you make?

TIPS FOR DRAMATIC ROLE PLAYS

- Decide who will take on the role of each character. You can also use a narrator for the introduction and the solution.
- Each character can write a few notes or prompts for his or her lines.
- Use props to create a realistic backdrop.
- Articulate clearly and with enthusiasm. Sell it!
- Don't stay frozen in one place. Move around.
- Use gestures.

X-Everything

Extreme Records

True or False?

1. Two different people hold the world record for sitting in a bathtub with 75 rattlesnakes.

2. An Australian set the record for pulling a 184-tonne airplane.

3. A Scottish woman has 720 **piercings** on her body, including 192 on her facial area.

4. An Englishman holds the world's **blindfold** motorcycle speed record. He drove his motorcycle at 265.33 km per hour while blindfolded.

5. A German set the record for the most consecutive skateboard front-side jumps off a **half-pipe**, doing 34 **ollies** in a row.

6. Four guys from Lévis, Québec, hold the record for the longest table football marathon at 35 hours and 11 minutes.

7. An Australian set the record for the longest drumming marathon, playing drums for 84 hours.

⊚ ASK YOURSELF …

What amazing world records do you know? What do you know about extreme jobs and extreme sports? What characteristics do extreme workers and athletes have?

Write down your ideas and opinions about these questions on your Action Plan sheet. ——————○

- With a partner, read the world records on this page.
- Together, decide which records you think are false. Which ones are true?
- Share your reactions with your classmates.
- Then, look at the illustrations on the next page. Match each picture with its **caption**.
- Which activity seems like the most fun?

Gl⊚ssary

caption = words written near a photo or illustration

piercings = holes made in the skin to attach jewellery

blindfold = piece of cloth used to covered the eyes

half-pipe = U-shaped ramp used by skateboarders

ollies = skateboard jumps

W⊚rd Wise

I think this record is …
There's no way that is true.
I can't believe that …
It's amazing to think that …

NOW, THAT'S EXCITEMENT!

1. **Now that's cool!**
   Watch your step as you make your way to the top.

2. **To the max!**
   Try **aerials**—it's the perfect sport for adrenaline addicts.

3. **Move till you drop**
   Get your adrenaline really pumping and show off your skill as you do a wall ride.

4. **Nature lovers, take note**
   Get ready to defy gravity as you ride furiously down the mountain tracks.

5. **Thrill-seekers wanted**
   For the thrill of a lifetime, jump at 4,000 metres for a 60-second free fall.

GlOssary

aerials = freestyle skiing jumps
till you drop = until you are exhausted
thrill-seekers = people looking for excitement and strong emotions

First

- Work with a partner.
- Look at the cartoon on this page.
- What message is the artist trying to give?
- Tell your partner what you think.

Next

- Read the text *Whatever It Takes*.
- What do you think the writer is trying to say?

Finally

- Read the text *Extreme Adventure in Pamplona* on page 113.
- Use strategies and resources as you read.
- What surprised you in the text?
- What do you think of the tradition of the Running of the Bulls?
- Talk it over with a partner. Share your opinions with the class.

Word Wise

I understood that …
It made me think that …
I believe the writer is trying to say that …

Glossary

break a record = do better than the current record
hazardous = dangerous
dash = run suddenly
brewery = beer factory
settle = end, decide

Extreme Times

Some people will do anything, no matter how extreme, to get into the *Guinness World Records Book*.

"Congratulations on smashing the marathon world record! What would you say was the secret to your success?

Whatever It Takes

Some people will do anything to **break a record**. One man sat watching television for almost 70 hours. He broke the previous record by over 20 hours. Now, that's pretty excessive.

5 The *Guinness World Records Book* has removed some records from its pages. Records about eating or drinking are no longer accepted. They are considered too dangerous for health reasons. Some stunts are also considered too extreme to be
10 included in the book. So don't go jumping out of an airplane without a parachute anytime soon. It's just too **hazardous**. You'll have better luck sitting in front of your TV, watching your favourite programs for a time—a very long time.

Extreme Adventure in Pamplona

Some people go on vacation to relax and go sightseeing. Others go for the adventure.

It's the third week of July in Pamplona, Spain. Anticipation is heavy in the air. It is quiet. Suddenly you hear voices shouting and the
5 sound of hooves. The noises become stronger. It's the Running of the Bulls!

People come rushing around the corner. They are pushing and shoving each other. If you look closely, you can see the excitement and fear in
10 their eyes. The running crowd is closely followed by six ferocious-looking bulls. People slip and jump and **dash** to escape.
15 You can't get more extreme than this.

People from all over the world turn up for the
20 Running of the Bulls, the annual festival in honour of the patron saint of Pamplona, San Fermin. They come in search of that rush of adrenalin. The event has grown in popularity over the last few years. And each year, more
25 people are hurt. The local Spaniards complain that the tourists make it more dangerous for the local bull runners. Still, if you want extreme excitement, nothing compares to Pamplona in July.

WOrd Wise

I found … surprising because …
I don't think I would …
What would you do if …?

First

- Explore the three texts on pages 114 and 115.

STRATEGY

Predict.
Look at the titles and pictures for cues that will help you deduce the subject of each text.

Next

- Form teams. Decide how you want to read the three texts.
  - You can work together on all three texts.
  - You can each read one text and tell each other what you learned.
  - You can read the three texts on your own and then compare your answers.
- Use the chart and questions on your activity sheet to help you understand and think about the texts.

Finally

- Which job do you think is the most dangerous?
- Which job would you be willing to do? Explain your choice.

Glossary

weak at heart = not courageous
remote = far way, isolated
skyscraper = very tall building that seems to touch the sky
girders = large metal construction supports
gridlocked = congested with traffic
dodge = evade

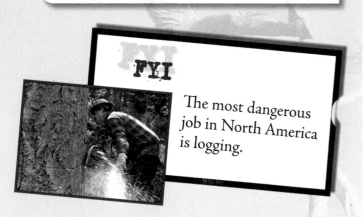

FYI

The most dangerous job in North America is logging.

Extreme Jobs

Some jobs are just not made for the **weak at heart**.

Smoke Jumper

My name is Daniel Cohen and I am a smoke jumper. I parachute into **remote** areas to fight fires. Once I land, I hike to the scene of the fire and begin the difficult task of putting it out. The work
5 is manual and physically exhausting. My job is one of the riskiest jobs out there. It is not only because I am fighting fires that it's dangerous but also because I have to parachute into the area.

This extreme job is different because I do not
10 immediately have control of the situation. That is what I am there to do. The most important thing to remember is to stay focused and not panic, no matter what happens. It is frightening at first, but experience helps me control the fear. I am always
15 aware of things like the wind, which can be disastrous for a fire fighter. If I stop paying attention for a second, the fire can quickly get out of control. That could cost me my life.

Sky Walkers

It is a sunny day but a little windy. I will have to be careful. The wind can be dangerous. My
5 name is Joe Fields and today I am working on the 53rd floor of a new **skyscraper** in Chicago. I guess that's pretty extreme. Still, the height doesn't bother me. I
10 come from a great line of Mohawk ironworkers. My family has worked on the highest buildings in North America. My great-grandfather was one of the legendary Skywalkers. In fact, my ancestors helped build some of the highest
15 skyscrapers in New York City, like the Empire State Building and the World Trade Centre.

Even when we are working on the tallest buildings, I never worry about falling. I worry about the weather. If it rains, the steel **girders**
20 become slippery, and walking them becomes more dangerous. If the wind suddenly changes direction, I could easily lose
25 my balance. It's important to be alert at all times. After all, my life depends on it.

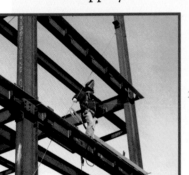

Ride Like the Wind

It's 8:30 in the morning and I'm already halfway downtown to pick up another package. My name is Hélène Salvani and I'm bicycle messenger #511. I deliver packages to different businesses throughout
5 the city. Each morning I go by the central office and they tell me where to go for my first delivery. I spend my day speeding from one client to the next. I am the fastest cyclist they have. In my job I need to be fast. I also need to know the city very well.
10 It's important to know which streets are **gridlocked**. Traffic jams are the most dangerous part of my job. Even the most careful cyclist can get hurt when drivers become impatient. I **dodge** cars, trucks and pedestrians all day as I
15 peddle from one place to another.

The weather is also a danger in my job. Rain and snow make the roads slippery. I have to keep an eye out for ice, falling pedestrians
20 and sliding cars. My day usually finishes at around 5:30 p.m. and I cycle home … slowly.

VOCABULARY

GRAMMAR WORKS

- The **superlative** form is used to compare three or more things. It indicates the highest level.

- To form the superlative, use **the** + adjective + **est** for adjectives of one syllable and most adjectives of two syllables.
     the tallest buildings   *the riskiest job*

- For adjectives of three or more syllables and adjectives of two syllables ending in **ful** or **re**, use **the most** + adjective.
     the most important thing   *the most careful cyclist*

First

● Before you read the text, share what you know about extreme sports and the X Games with the class.

Next

● Read the text, then scan it to answer the following questions.
  1. Why do athletes go to the X Games?
  2. What extreme sport is the author talking about?
  3. What arguments are given against extreme sports?
  4. Why does the writer disagree?

Then

● Look at the verbs in the text. What tense are they?

● Why do you think the writer uses that verb tense to talk about the event?

Finally

● Look at the illustrations on the next page.

● Which statement best describes your reaction to each picture, A or B?

● Read your extreme personality profile.

● Tell your partner if you agree with your profile.

WOrd Wise

I don't agree with …
That is exactly like me because …
That really isn't me because …
I think I'm more …

GlOssary

hook turn = a fast turn close to the ground
flip = turn over
down-to-earth = practical

Extreme Fun

Each year there are Olympic-style competitions called the X Games. They are held in different cities throughout the United States each year. However, the participants all share certain personality traits: they are young and like intense activities.

THE X GAMES

by Michael Landry

It's a sunny day in June. The young athletes are all lined up. They are cheerfully chatting with each other. These athletes are not really competing against one another. They are
5 competing against their own limits. Welcome to the X Games, where highly competitive people come to play.

It is here that dedicated athletes show what they can do in extreme sports. They defy
10 gravity and push the boundaries of regular sports. One enthusiastic athlete rapidly descends the ramp and does an extremely fast **hook turn** with his board. The adrenalin rush is there.

15 Some people might argue that extreme sports are not really athletic. They say that extreme sports are too dangerous. I disagree. Just come to the X Games. The organizers take many precautions to ensure the safety of all
20 the people involved. Here, the athletes take only calculated risks even if they push themselves to the limit. Tell me, what is more athletic than that?

DO YOU HAVE AN X PERSONALITY?

1

a) I prefer flying in an airplane.
b) Wow! I love this feeling.

2

a) I like to keep my board on the snow.
b) I could do a 540° **flip** on the way down.

3

a) I think I'm going to be sick.
b) What a great view from here!

4

a) Oh no, I'm stuck!
b) What a challenge!

5

a) If we were meant to fly, we would have wings!
b) Now, this is freedom.

6

a) If I close my eyes, I'll be fine.
b) Awesome! I wonder what it's like at night?

EXTREME PERSONALITY PROFILE

Mostly As:
You have a **down-to-earth** personality. No extreme risks for you. You are practical and sensible. You don't need an adrenalin rush to have fun.

Mostly Bs:
Your nickname is X because you like all things extreme. Remember, you can also have fun without getting your heart pumping so hard.

Adjectives and Adverbs

1 **Show what you know.**

- Find two adjectives and two adverbs in these sentences from the text *The X Games*.

  The young athletes are all lined up. They are cheerfully chatting with each other. Welcome to the X Games, where highly competitive people come to play.

- Which words do the adjectives describe? Which words do the adverbs modify?

2 **Review adjectives.**

- Adjectives are used to describe a noun or a pronoun.

- Adjectives are usually placed before the noun:

     adj.   **noun**
  Great athletes learn by practising.

- Adjectives are placed after the verbs *to be, to become* and *to seem*. These verbs link the adjective to the noun or pronoun it is describing:

     noun   *adj.*   **pronoun**   *adj.*
  Their tricks may <u>seem</u> *easy* but they <u>are</u> *difficult* to do.

  In English, an adjective has no gender and is never plural:
  An *enthusiastic* boy, an *enthusiastic* girl, *enthusiastic* competitors

- However, some adjectives are more commonly used for females, others for males:
  a *pretty* girl, a *beautiful* woman, a *handsome* man

3 **Review adverbs.**

- An adverb can modify a verb. The adverb is usually placed after the direct object but its position can vary, depending on the type of adverb.

     verb   **object** *adv.*   *adv.*   **verb**
  He plays the piano *well*. He *usually* practises three hours a day.

- An adverb can modify an adjective. The adverb is placed before the adjective.

     adv.   **adj.**   **noun**
  That is a *really* difficult trick.

- An adverb can modify another adverb. The adverbs are placed one after the other.

     verb *adv.*   *adv.*
  He turned *very smoothly*.

- An adverb can modify a complete sentence. The adverb is usually placed at the beginning of the sentence.

     adv.
  Unfortunately, he did not break the world record.

4 Adjective or adverb?

- Adverbs of manner answer the question "How?"
- Many adjectives can become adverbs of manner by adding **ly**:
  Suzie is an attentive listener. She listens attentive**ly**. (How does she listen?)
  Carlos is a cautious climber. He climbs cautious**ly**. (How does Carlos climb?)
- There are some exceptions:

Adjective	◆	Adverb	
good	◆	well	Lynne is a good swimmer. She swims **well**.
hard	◆	hard	Miriam is a hard worker. She works **hard**.
fast	◆	fast	Marcos is a fast driver. He drives **fast**.

For more on adjectives and adverbs, go to page 198.

5 Practise.

A. Go back to the text *The X Games* on page 116 and find three other adverbs and three other adjectives.
- Write them in your notebook.
- Compare your answers with a partner.

B. Read the following article.
- Decide which of the words in parentheses (adjective or adverb) should be used.
- Write your answers in your notebook.

A (true / truly) unbelievable event happened recently. An Englishman set an (amazing / amazingly) world record by balancing a 159.6 kg car on his head for 33 seconds. This was (extreme /extremely) dangerous, even for John Evans. Evans has made a career out of balancing (different / differently) objects on his head. He (regular / regularly) balances items such as books or canned drinks. He even (occasion / occasionally) balances people. He has also put 101 house bricks on his head: the bricks weighed an (incredible / incredibly) 188.6 kg. Balancing a car has been Evans' most (intense / intensely) **feat** yet. He is able to balance (heavy / heavily) things on his head because he has such a (strong / strongly) neck: it measures 60.9 cm.

Gl**o**ssary

feat = exploit, accomplishment

First

- Explore the text by looking at the title and picture and skimming the text to get an idea of its content.
- What do they tell you about the text?
- How is this text different from the text *The X Games* on page 116?

STRATEGY

Compare.
Compare two similar texts to become aware of the similarities and differences in their structure and content.

Next

- Read the text carefully. Use strategies and resources as you read.
- Answer the following questions:
  1. What event does the text describe?
  2. Where is the writer during the event?
  3. The title *Triumph* refers to two things. What do you think they are?

Finally

- Look at the structure of the text *Triumph*.
  - Is the tone heavy or light?
  - In general, are the sentences long or short?
  - Is the opinion of the writer obvious?
  - Are the descriptions clear?
- Keep these questions in mind for when you write a descriptive report of your own.

◉ ASK YOURSELF ...

What do you think now?

Look at the notes you wrote on your Action Plan sheet at the beginning of the unit. Is there anything you have changed your mind about? Do you have any new ideas? Write them down in part 2.

Glossary

burst = short, sudden effort
alike = in the same way, both

Live from the Scene

Triumph

This year's annual mountain bike competition is a great success. There are many motivated competitors and the crowds are enthusiastic. The courses here are long and tough. They really test the abilities
5 and determination of the riders. What an extreme show!

The athletes have worked hard to get to the finals. This competition is their ultimate test. I am waiting at the finish line. I love the anticipation.
10 As a spectator, the thrill is waiting to see who comes over the hill first.

There is a loud shout. Suddenly I see the first rider. Her number is 9396. She is pedalling furiously as she nears the finish line. There is a second rider
15 close behind. The race is still on. The first rider gives a final **burst** of speed. The crowd cheers excitedly. Rider number 9396 crosses the finish line first, her arms in the air. The fans applaud and shout their congratulations.

20 It has been a tiring day for the competitors, but great fun. Winners and losers **alike** have had a good time. And for those who didn't win, well, there is always next year.

VOCABULARY

LANGUAGE WORKS

Talking about Capabilities and Preferences

1 Look at the following language models.

Capabilities
I know how to …
We might be able to …
I'm sure that we are capable of …

Preferences
Which record do you want to try for?
I would rather try for that record.
Which would you prefer?

STRATEGY

Remember you can use strategies to aid communication. See pages 205–207 for a complete list of strategies.

2 Form teams.

- List other ways for expressing capabilities and preferences in your notebook. Use them during your discussion when you can.

3 Listen to the conversation.

- Listen to the conversation some students are having about Record Week at their school.
- Pay attention to the language they use to express capabilities and preferences.
- Write down a few examples as you listen.

4 Decide which record your class or school should try to set.

- Look at the suggestions for setting a record. With your group, choose one activity that you think you could do at your school.
- Decide how you will organize the activity and who will be involved. Reach an agreement on when and where this activity will take place. Present your decisions to your classmates.

SELF-CHECK

☑ Think about the strategies you used. Which ones were most helpful to you? Which ones will you try to use the next time you interact orally?

Suggestions
- Longest musical concert
- Largest number of books stacked in a column in a designated time
- Tallest sculpture inside a gym
- Longest distance hopped on one foot by 100 students
- Painting of the longest mural by the most students
- Longest human chain of students holding hands around a school building
- Longest basketball or volleyball match
- Your suggestion

Write On

◎ YOUR TASK

Write a descriptive report about one of these topics:
• an extreme sports event
• a record-breaking event

Your article will contain:
• a strong opening paragraph setting the scene
• a separate paragraph each for
  – a description of the event
  – your reaction and the reaction of the crowd at the event
  – your opinion of the event
• a conclusion that summarizes the major points ———○

❶ Plan your writing.

- Look at the models on pages 113, 116 and 120. Use the same structure for your text.
- Think about the things you learned in this unit about extreme events.
- Look at your Action Plan notes and the texts in the unit for ideas.
- Do some research at the library or on the Internet and take notes.
- Use a graphic organizer to organize your thoughts. ••••••••••••••••••••••••

❷ Write a first draft of your text.

- Look at your graphic organizer to help you write about the different components.
- Use new words from your vocabulary log.

❸ Revise and edit your text.

- Add, substitute, delete and rearrange ideas and words.
- Add a title to your text.
- Edit your text using your checklist and other resources as needed.
- Ask someone to check your work.
- Write your final copy.

❹ Go public.

- Share your text with the class.

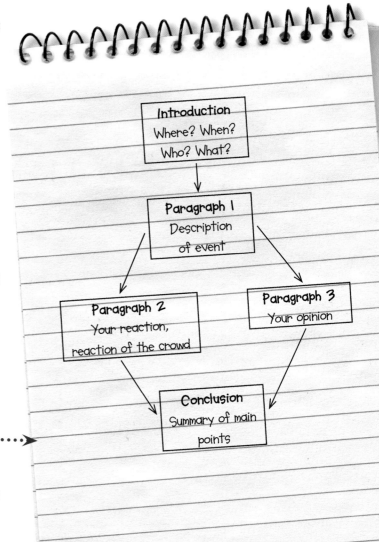

Introduction
Where? When? Who? What?

↓

Paragraph 1
Description of event

Paragraph 2
Your reaction, reaction of the crowd

Paragraph 3
Your opinion

Conclusion
Summary of main points

Give your article an interesting title.

EXTREMELY ENERGIZING BASKETBALL MARATHON

Grab your reader's attention with a descriptive first paragraph.

The lights are on. The Phys. Ed. teacher is giving us some last-minute instructions. The students are listening attentively. It is a sunny Saturday morning and we are all in the school gym. The challenge is on to set the world record for the longest-running basketball match.

In the body of your text, use adjectives and adverbs to describe the event from your point of view.

At first, I am excited. I really like basketball so this shouldn't be too hard. After two long hours I'm extremely tired ...

Many enthusiastic parents have come to support their kids. They cheer us on loudly ...

In your conclusion, wrap up your main points.

What a great way to spend my weekend ...
The crowd was great ...
Mission accomplished ...

UNIT 11

To Work or Not to Work

That Is the Question

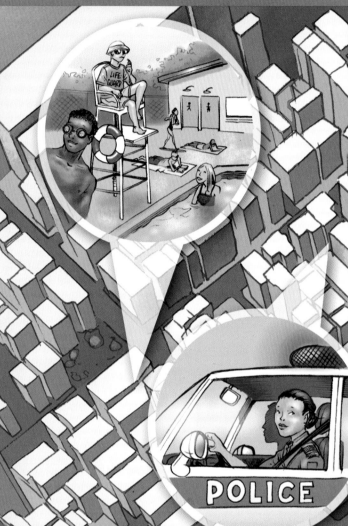

◎ **ASK YOURSELF …**

Are you planning to look for a summer job? Do you know what skills and qualities you have to offer? Do you know how to write a cover letter and a CV? Write down your thoughts about these questions on your Action Plan sheet.

- Look at the city map.
- Answer the following questions about paid work and volunteer work:
  - Find two places where teenagers can do volunteer work.
  - Find three places with popular jobs for teenagers. What are the names of these jobs? Would you spend your summer doing any of these jobs?
  - Find two jobs teenagers cannot do.
  - Which job on the map would you like the most? the least?
  - What are some other jobs that are popular for teenagers where you live?

Word Wise

I would like to work as a …
I wouldn't like to …
Teenagers can work as a …
Teens can't work as a …
  lifeguard
  animal caretaker
  police officer
  care giver (for the elderly)
  camp counsellor
  doctor
I could …
  pick berries
  mow lawns

CV is an abbreviation for curriculum vitae, Latin for "course of life." CVs are used to tell the reader what skills, qualities and experience you have to offer. They are requested when you apply for a job and even for volunteer work. A CV is sometimes called a resumé.

First

- In your notebook draw a chart like the one in the next column.
- Write down all the **pros** and **cons** you can think of for having a summer job.

STRATEGY

Pay selective attention.
Decide to concentrate on finding specific pieces of information in the texts.

Next

- As you read, circle all the pros and cons in your chart that are mentioned in the text.
- Add to your chart any new pros and cons from the texts.

Finally

- Do you think there are more pros or cons to working part time?
- Would you consider getting a part-time job?

What's in a WOrd?

Words that have similar spelling and have the same meaning in English and French are called cognates. If they have similar spelling but their meanings are different, they are called false cognates.

If you are not sure of the meaning of a word, use a dictionary.

Are the following words cognates or false cognates?

MATURE   BALANCE   BUDGET

ISSUE   ARGUMENT

GlOssary

pros = reasons supporting a side in a debate
cons = reasons against a side in a debate

A Summer Job: Should I, Could I?

Summer is soon upon us. Many of you will try to find your first summer job or return to a previous one. Some of you might have a part-time job already and want to work more hours during the summer. Read the following blog messages and decide if getting a summer job is a good idea for you.

Getting a summer job	
Pros	Cons
I can make money.	I will have less free time.
I can meet new people.	

FYI

You need to know your Québec work laws. If you are under 14, you must have a parent or guardian's written consent if you wish to work. And you can't work during the day when you are required to attend school.

In the last issue of *Community Corner*, I asked parents and teenagers to tell me whether they thought summer jobs for teenagers were a good thing or not. With summer just around the corner, the response was incredible. Here are some of the messages I received. ●

Marc

Hi Marc,

I think that getting a job was the best thing that could have happened to my daughter. She was very, very shy and she had a hard time making
5 friends. I encouraged her to get a summer job at the local community camp. It changed her life. Now she **gets along** with everyone, and she has a lot more **self-confidence**. In fact, she just joined the theatre club at school. She
10 even says that she wants to work with children in the future. I say that a summer job is the best way to go. ●

Michelle
Posted April 12 4:15

15 Dear Marc,

I won't let my two teenagers work. I am afraid that if they start working and make some money, they will drop out of school and never go back. My brother got a job in high school and
20 has worked at low-paying jobs ever since. He never finished school. I think education is the way to **get ahead** in life. The way I see it, you have a lifetime to work. Teenagers should just be teenagers and focus on their studies. ●

25 David
Posted April 17 9:05

Marc,

I was tired of always asking my parents for money and wanted to show them that I was
30 responsible. So I got a summer job at the mall. I worked enough hours to buy all my own clothes. I even learned to budget. When school started again in the fall, my parents told me I could work weekends as long as my grades
35 didn't suffer. I think that's a fair deal. ●

Sarah
Posted April 23 11:22

Hello Marc,

I had a summer job that I kept part-time when
40 school started again. At first I was able to handle both, but then I **got behind** in my school work. My grades started to go down and I was always tired. My mother told me that I had to quit my job, so I did. The following school year
45 I tried working again and it went OK. I think that if you can find a balance between your job and school, then working is a great experience. My different jobs helped me decide what to study in CEGEP. ●

50 Kim
Posted May 6 10:09

VOCABULARY

Glossary

gets along = is friends with
self-confidence = a good feeling about yourself
get ahead = to be successful
got behind = was late doing something

First

- Look at the two logos on pages 128 and 129. In your notebook, write what you know about the organizations they represent.

Next

- Read the four texts, using strategies and resources to understand new words and expressions.
- Use the chart on your reading log to organize the information.

Finally

- Answer the questions in the reading log.
- Compare your answers with a partner.

GRAMMAR WORKS

Nouns as adjectives

Sometimes a noun acts as an adjective, describing the noun that follows it.

For example: *The first animal shelter opened in Montréal in 1928.*

animal and *shelter* are both nouns but *animal* is a noun-as-adjective because it describes the noun *shelter*.

Glossary

CSPCA = Canadian Society for the Prevention of Cruelty to Animals

A Canadian Tradition

Volunteering is a great way to get real work experience and help others too! Read about some of the best-known Canadian volunteering organizations.

For Our Four-Legged Friends

The Canadian Society for the Prevention of Cruelty to Animals was founded in Montréal in 1869. At that time, farmers
5 used horses to work on the land. At first, the goal of the organization was to make sure that the owners did not beat their horses and that they fed them well. Later, the **CSPCA** and its volunteers expanded its
10 mandate to make sure that all animals were treated correctly. The first CSPCA animal shelter opened in Montréal in 1928. ●

For Our Youth and Communities

Katimavik was established by the Honourable Jacques Hébert in 1977. The aim of this non-profit organization is to help young Canadians develop their leadership skills. To do
5 this, they take part in volunteer projects. The organization forms work camps of 11 people and sends them to different areas throughout Canada. Each volunteer works 35 hours a week with a group on various tasks. Volunteers might
10 be asked to work with the elderly or the mentally challenged, or they might have to do more physical work, such as cleaning up park paths or collecting recycled material. ●

For Our Country

Canada has always been ready to help people in need. In fact, Canada's first charitable organization was founded in Québec in 1639. Immigrants **went through** a lot of hardship
5 when they first arrived in Québec, but in that year, they faced a **plague**, too. It was the nurses at Hôtel Dieu who **lent a hand**. Later, in 1688, Monseigneur Laval created an organisation of volunteers who collected
10 money, food and clothing for the poor. This was the beginning of the development of many volunteer and charitable organisations in Québec and throughout Canada. ●

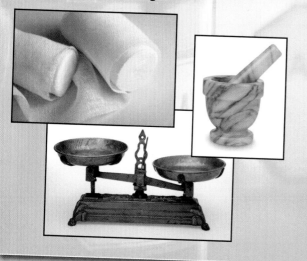

⬭ VOCABULARY ⬭

Gl⊙ssary

went through = endured, experienced
plague = a deadly contagious disease
lent a hand = helped others by giving food, medicine and shelter
needy = poor, without essentials for daily life

For Our Sick and Needy

In 1885, during the Louis Riel Rebellion, Dr. George Sterling Ryerson used a red cross on his ambulance as he traversed enemy lines. He got the idea from Henri Dunant, the founder of the Red Cross
5 organisation in Switzerland 22 years earlier. The red cross stood for neutrality and allowed Dr. Ryerson to transport injured people off the battlefield. Then, in 1896, Dr. Ryerson officially formed the first overseas division of the British Red Cross This became the
10 Canadian Red Cross 10 years later. The mission of the Canadian Red Cross is to help people in need due to catastrophes and natural disasters. In Canada, the Red Cross has played an important role in hospitals in remote areas of the country and offers popular
15 swimming and first-aid courses. ●

 Canadian Red Cross

First

- Take the quiz in the next column. Answer yes or no to each question.

Next

- Total your score. Count how many yes answers you have and see if you are ready to get a job.

Finally

- Did the results of the quiz surprise you? Tell a partner why or why not.

Gl⊙ssary

keep your cool = stay calm, not get angry
punctual = on time
keep up with = do (it) on time
suitable = appropriate

Ready to Work?

Getting a job is a huge responsibility that teenagers can handle if they have reached a certain level of maturity. See how ready you are to work by taking this quiz.

1. Do you listen carefully to instructions?

2. Do you usually complete a task once you start it?

3. Can you make decisions on your own?

4. Do you learn from your mistakes?

5. Do you get along with people of all ages?

6. Do you **keep your cool** when someone criticizes your work?

7. Are you **punctual**?

8. Are you able to **keep up with** your school work?

9. Are your clothes and appearance **suitable** for the workplace?

10. Are you able to get up on time without help from a parent?

How ready are you?

1–4 yes answers = Maybe you should start with a part-time summer job.

5–8 yes answers = You are ready, but talk to friends and family for some personal pointers.

9–10 yes answers = Start handing out your CV! You are definitely ready!

LANGUAGE WORKS

Expressing Interests and Preferences

1 Look at the following language models.

> Which would you prefer?
> Wouldn't you rather …?
> I would like to …
> I can't stand …
> I enjoy …
> Do you enjoy …?
> Would you like …?
> Given the choice, I'd …
> I don't mind …
> They would rather …

STRATEGY

Remember you can use strategies to aid communication. See pages 205–207 for a complete list of strategies.

2 **Form teams.**

- Practise using the language models given in the box. Brainstorm other ways that you know to express interests and preferences.

3 **Listen to the conversation.** 🎧

- Some students are discussing their interests and whether they want to work during the summer or not.
- Pay attention to the language they use to express their interests and preferences.
- Write down a few example as you listen.
- Listen again to the recording and answer the questions on your activity sheet.

SELF-CHECK

✔️ Think about the strategies you used. Which ones were most helpful to you? Which ones will you try to use the next time you interact orally?

4 **Talk about your preferences.**
Are you planning to work this summer?

- With your team, discuss whether you want to work during the summer or not.
- Give reasons to support your answer.
- Then, come to a consensus on whether or not high-school teens should get a summer job.

First
- Read the tips for writing a good cover letter and CV.

Next
- Read the job posting.

Camp Counselor

Do you love working with children? Do you have a lot of energy? Do you like playing sports, cooking and doing **crafts**?

Why not apply at Happy Hands and Feet for a camp counsellor job. Previous experience with children aged 5–9 is an asset. The position is available from June until August. The **hourly rate** is negotiable.

Send your CV to the Seaside Community Centre.

- Read Stephanie's and Sam's cover letters and CVs on page 133.
- As you read each cover letter and CV, check off the criteria you find in the chart on your activity sheet.

Then
- Review the criteria to help you decide who has written a better cover letter and CV.
- What needs to be changed or added in each cover letter and CV?
- Share your answers with a partner.

Finally
- In your opinion, who is more qualified for the job, Stephanie or Sam? Discuss this with your partner.

Gl☺ssary
crafts = art projects
hourly rate = money paid per hour

CV and Me!

Have you ever been to a grocery store or pharmacy and noticed the job boards? Posted on these boards are all types of jobs for all types of people.

A good cover letter has
- the date
- the name and address of the place of business you are applying to
- the name of the job or specific position you are applying for
- an explanation about why you would be good for the job
- your signature

A good CV
- has contact information such as your address and phone number
- states your level of education
- lists special classes you have taken (for example, art, music, karate)
- lists the languages you speak or are learning
- lists work or volunteer work experience (if possible)
- lists your skills and qualities (for example, organized, artistic)
- mentions any special awards received
- contains no spelling or grammar errors

A

Seaside Community Centre
727 Pleasant Lane
Petersville, Nova Scotia
B9L 2S4

To whom it may concern:

I am interested in your camp counsellor position. I feel that I have the qualities and skills that you are looking for. I have a lot of experience with children. I am very reliable and energetic. I love playing sports and singing songs.

I hope to receive a favourable response from you.

Yours truly,
Stephanie Aboud

B

June 02, 20XX

Seaside Community Centre
727 Pleasant Lane
Petersville, Nova Scotia
B9L 2S4

Dear Sirs,

As you can see from my CV, I have a lot of experience. My tutoring work will help make me a good camp counsellor.
I enjoy spending time outdoors and I can help children with their computer skills.

I hope you will give me a call.

Sincerely,
Sam Romero

C

Stephanie Aboud
545 Applewood Street
Waterway, Nova Scotia B9L 9G2
(444) 444-4444

Education & Classes:
- Heritage High School, Petersville, Nova Scotia, Secondary III
- Babysitting training, Seaside Community Centre
- Singing classes, Sound of Angels Academy
- Lifeguard courses, Seaside Community Centre

Languages Spoken:
- French, English and Spanish

Work Experience:
- Babysitting for the past six years
- Dog walker
- Running errands for elderly neighbours

Volunteer Work:
- Reading books to seniors at Waterway Retirement Home

Awards:
- Goalie of the year for soccer

D

Sam Romero
624 Hillcrest Road
Petersville, Nova Scotia B9L 2T4
(555) 555-5555

Experience
Math tutor for Homework Helpers at Parkside
Elementary School, grades 2–4
Dog walker for family and friends all year
round for the past seven years
Mowed lawns in the neighbourhood for the past five years

Background
Heritage High School, Petersville, N.S.
currently in Secondary III
Kicking Karate Korner School, Petersville
working toward a black belt
CPR class at Heritage High School
Lifeguard courses at YMCA

Computer Skills
Basic computer skills
create web pages

Other Skills
Excellent chess player
Very hard worker

Some Unusual Jobs

Some people actually have these unusual jobs.

- Tell a partner what you think of the following jobs.
  - Which job would you enjoy the most?
  - Which one would you never do?
  - Which ones do you think are strange, disgusting or dangerous?

Read about some disgusting, strange and dangerous jobs. The next time you complain that you have to clean your room or wash the dishes, think about how those **chores** compare to these jobs.

Odour Judge

Odour judges are employed in research labs. **In a nutshell**, their job consists of smelling things and judging the smells. For example, mouthwash companies use odour judges to
5 determine how effective their product is. Test subjects with disgusting, vile breath blow in the faces of the judges and then blow again after using mouthwash. Odour judges also smell armpits and smelly shoes to test whether
10 deodorants are effective.

Glossary

chores = routine household tasks
in a nutshell = in a few words
up close and personal = in direct contact, directly
fine-tuned = precise

Volcanologist

Volcanologists have one of the hottest jobs on earth—lava temperatures can reach an incredible 1200 degrees Celsius. Though they spend much of their time in the laboratory, volcanologists

5 also spend two to three months living in a tent next to a volcano 10 so they can record data **up close and personal.**

Golf Ball Diver

Believe it or not, people earn a living diving into lakes and ponds on golf courses to retrieve golf balls. They wear a wet suit and scuba gear to do the job right. The golf balls are then shipped to 5 refinishing companies that sell the golf balls for half the price of new balls.

Foot Model

Do you like your feet? Some people have such nice feet that they model them for a living. A foot model can earn up to $300 an hour. To prepare for such a job, you have to have 5 smooth and well-pedicured feet. Foot models put a lot of cream on their feet and cover them with plastic bags before going to sleep. These models almost never wear 10 high-heeled shoes— they can deform the feet.

Face Feeler

A face what? That's right, it's somebody's job to feel people's faces. Face feelers have a very **fine-tuned** sense of touch. They feel people's faces for companies that sell razors and lotions, 5 for example. A face feeler can feel whether a razor gives a man a smooth shave and if lotions make people's skin feel soft.

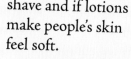

Dog Food Tester

Don't all dogs deserve to eat tasty food? That's why dog food testers eat the dog food themselves. If it's tasty and moist enough for a human, then it might be just perfect for a dog.

VOCABULARY

 ASK YOURSELF ...

What do you think now?

Look at the notes you wrote on your Action Plan sheet at the beginning of the unit. Is there anything you have changed your mind about? Do you have any new ideas? Write them down in part 2.

Problematic Prepositions

1 **Show what you know.**
- Find all of the prepositions of time or position in the following text.
- Write them in your notebook, indicating T for time or P for position beside each one.

I start my first job in one hour. I am very nervous but also excited. I will be working at a bakery for three months. I love cooking so I think it's the perfect job for me. Last week I had a training session at the bakery. I learned how to put icing on the pastries. My schedule is pretty good, too. I start work every day at 9:00 a.m. and I finish at 3:00 p.m. so I still get to see my friends a lot.

2 **Review prepositions of time and position.**

The preposition **in** is used to refer to an amount of time or to an enclosed space:
- I start my job **in** one hour.
- I work as a camp counsellor **in** the summer.

Phillip is **in** the interview room now.

My CV is **in** my briefcase.

The preposition **on** is used to refer to a surface or an area that is not enclosed:
- The candidates are eating lunch **on** the park bench.
- There is an application **on** the desk.

The preposition **on** is also used to refer to a specific day or date:
- They have a meeting **on** Monday.
- I start work **on** July 17.

The preposition **at** is used to refer to a location or a point in time:
- My sister is **at** a job interview now.
- My interview is **at** 10:00 a.m.

The preposition **for** is used to refer to a period of time:
- I waited for the interview to start **for** 30 minutes.

For more on problematic prepositions, go to page 201.

3 **Practise.**
- Use the prepositions *in, on, at* and *for* to describe what is happening in this picture. Write as many sentences as possible.
- Decide if the prepositions you used in your description are prepositions of time or location.

Write On

◎ YOUR TASK

Write a CV and cover letter for a summer job of your choice.

Your cover letter and CV will contain all the criteria listed for a good cover letter and CV on page 132. ————————————●

1 **Plan your writing.**

- Choose one of the jobs in the Summer Jobs box or another summer job you know about.
- Look at the cover letter models on page 133. Use the same structure for your cover letter.
- Take notes about
  – the job you want to apply for
  – why you want the job
  – why you would be good at the job
- Look at the CV models on page 133. Use the same structure for your CV.
- Take notes about
  – your level of education
  – any special classes you've taken
  – the languages you speak or are learning
  – your work experience
  – your volunteer experience
  – your skills
  – any awards or prizes you have won

2 **Write a first draft of your text.**

- Look at your notes to help you write your cover letter and CV in a logical order.
- Use new words from your vocabulary log.

3 **Revise and edit your text.**

- Add, substitute, delete and rearrange ideas and words.
- Edit your cover letter and CV using your checklists and other resources as needed.
- Ask someone to check your work.
- Write your final copies.

4 **Go public.**

- Show your cover letter and CV to an adult. What was their first impression?

SUMMER JOBS

- animal caretaker
- assistant soccer coach
- berry picker
- camp counsellor
- clothing store assistant
- fast-food server
- gardener's helper
- grocery store helper
- lifeguard
- mother's helper
- salesperson at a music store
- server at an ice cream shop
- swimming instructor
- ticket taker at an amusement park
- ticket taker at a movie complex

Project: Classy Magazine

Looking at You

◎ ANSWER THIS ...

In the past two units, you have become aware of your personality and looked at the world of work and occupations.

Now, at the end of this school year, can you produce an honest portrait of yourself—the real you—to share with your classmates?

Your personality type

- Look at the five topics on this page and think about what you are going to say.
- Discuss these topics with a classmate.

Your hobbies and interests

Your favourite subjects at school

Jobs that you find interesting

W**O**rd Wise

I think I am ...
   outgoing
   easy-going
   shy
   friendly

I would like to become a ...
What about you?
I'm not sure.

What you hope you will be doing in five years

YOUR PROJECT

Write and design a creative personal profile about yourself for a year-end class magazine. Present your profile to the class.

- Think about these questions.
  1. Have you ever been involved in making a class magazine?
  2. What do class magazines usually contain?
  3. What characteristics do they have?
  4. What sort of texts do they contain?

- The personal profiles contributed by students are a key feature of successful class magazines.

- Here are some of the characteristics of an effective personal profile for a class magazine.

CHARACTERISTICS OF AN EFFECTIVE PERSONAL PROFILE FOR A CLASS MAGAZINE

Follow these steps to create an effective and interesting profile:

1. Describe yourself. Don't be shy. Tell it like it is.

I guess I am an **outgoing** person. I have lots of friends. I am **involved** in many activities at school …

2. Tell your readers about an important event in your past.

Last September was quite an experience. I was the new kid in school. For the first two weeks, no one spoke to me except for the teachers. Then Sabrina started talking to me …

3. Describe your future plans and hopes.

This summer, I am going to work at a fast-food restaurant. I will have to study harder next year because I would like to go to CEGEP and university. I hope to move to a big city …

4. Add some visual impact to your profile with personal photos, drawings, symbols or slogans.

This is my favourite symbol. It represents …

Glossary

tell it like it is = be honest
outgoing = friendly and active
involved = taking part

First

- Look carefully at the three pages from a class magazine on pages 141, 142 and 143.
- Analyze the magazine and answer the questions.
  1. What grabs your attention first?
  2. What do you notice about the photos?
  3. Who is the classroom magazine written for?
  4. Are the language and visuals suitable for this audience?
  5. Are the type size and font appropriate?

Then

- With a partner, analyze the personal profiles on pages 2 and 3 of the magazine.
- Complete the chart on your activity sheet.
- Make an overall evaluation of the magazine.

Finally

- Share your analysis and evaluation of the magazine pages with another pair of students.
- Together, decide which personal profile is more effective, Nick's or Ariel's.
- Be prepared to explain the reasons for your choice.

Analysis of the personal profiles		
	Nick	**Ariel**
1. Is the visual design of the profile creative?	☐ Yes ☐ No	☐ Yes ☐ No
2. Is the content of the profile interesting?	☐ Yes ☐ No	☐ Yes ☐ No
3. Does the writer give enough details about his/her personality and interests?	☐ Yes ☐ No	☐ Yes ☐ No
4. Does the writer give enough details about a past event and future plans?	☐ Yes ☐ No	☐ Yes ☐ No
5. Is the personal slogan or motto meaningful?	☐ Yes ☐ No	☐ Yes ☐ No
6. Does the logo go with his/her personality?	☐ Yes ☐ No	☐ Yes ☐ No
7. Is the profile appropriate for a Secondary III class magazine?	☐ Yes ☐ No	☐ Yes ☐ No
Evaluation of the profiles		
Content	/10	/1
Presentation	/10	/1

WOrd Wise

This magazine is …
The profile on the second page is …
The pictures are …
The text is …
  clear
  easy to understand
  nicely done
  attractive
  funny
  professional-looking
  (not) original
  (not) very interesting

GlOssary

fundraising = event to collect money for a charity

THE HEROES OF HOMEROOM 311

**Written by and for the students of Group 311,
Secondary III, Bouchard Academy**

Scary Halloween Creatures

Winter Carnival

Fundraising

On Stage

Our Teachers

Nick Arsenault

I am a **down-to-earth**, easy-going guy. I guess I'm a **loner** because I have a couple of friends but not many. My hobbies include playing video games and making home movies. I also collect movies that have extraordinary special effects, like *King Kong* and *Lord of the Rings*. I am really **into** how special effects are made. I have a lot of fun trying to create special effects with my **camcorder**. I don't belong to any sports teams but I exercise at home in a homemade gym in my basement.

Motto: I'll get there in the end.

Something happened at Christmas that really changed my life. I spent time with my father for the first time in five years. It seems my father had a lot of problems when he left my mother and me. My mother is a hard-working and courageous person. She made sure I had everything I needed, even with my father gone. So, on Boxing Day, he showed up and took me out for a nice meal. He took me shopping, too: he bought me a professional photography light. He is now sending me a monthly allowance and he says he will help me with my studies. I am happy to have my father back in my life again.

I did not have many plans for the future before. But now, with two parents **pulling for me**, many things are possible. I am going to start private lessons in Math to get better results. This summer I want to get a summer job. If all goes well (and it will), I'll go to CEGEP in two years. After that, I'll have to choose a university. I am not quite sure what to study yet, maybe communication arts and how to produce TV shows and make movies. In 10 years, I could even be a father. Imagine that!

Glossary

down-to-earth = realistic
loner = person who likes to be alone
into = interested in
camcorder = portable video camera
pulling for me = wanting me to be successful

Ariel Blanchet

I am a very dynamic kind of person. I am always **on the go**. I'm a people person. I play volleyball for the school team. I also play hockey for the city team. I'm the goalie. When I have the time, I really go in for extreme sports like mountain biking and skateboarding.

My motto is **LIVE LIFE TO THE MAX**.

During the March break, I went on a trip to Mexico with my parents. What an experience! We spent a few days in Cancun, the capital of the Mayan Riviera. The beaches are beautiful. We even did some snorkeling around the reefs. After **taking it easy** for a few days, we were ready to visit the rest of the Yucatan Peninsula. We went to see the Mayan ruins at Chichen Itza: what remarkable buildings, right there in the middle of the tropical forest! Then we spent a half-day at Tulum to visit more Mayan ruins, but this time right on the ocean. We stayed a few days at Playa del Carmen before heading home. I realized that the world has many interesting places to see.

Chichen Itza

Tulum

I plan to work at a sports store this summer. My experience with all kinds of sports will **come in handy**. I know that I am going to study hard so I can have an interesting career. I want a job where I can work with people: teacher, psychologist or something like that. I am also going to travel a lot. I hope to try something cool in every place I visit, such as rock climbing or **trekking**.

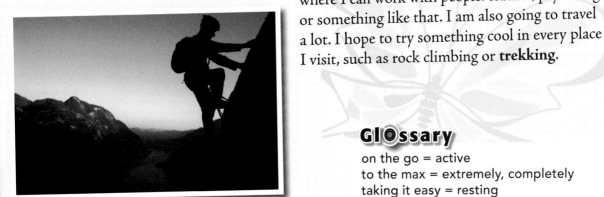

Gl☺ssary

on the go = active
to the max = extremely, completely
taking it easy = resting
come in handy = be useful
trekking = long walks through mountains and difficult terrain

Producing a Class Magazine

❶ PREPRODUCTION

● **Plan your project.**

- Design a personal profile about yourself for a class magazine.
- Use pages 2 and 3 of the *Heroes of Homeroom 311* class magazine as models.
- Get ideas for content in Units 10 and 11.
- If computers are available, search the Internet for design and illustration ideas.
- Refer to the characteristics of effective personal profiles on page 139.
- Your personal profile should contain at least three sections.
- Decide on the design of your profile.
- Find visuals to complement your text: photos, drawings, logos, etc.

❷ PRODUCTION

● **Prepare a first draft.**

- Write the first draft using appropriate language.
- Choose effective vocabulary to write a clear and original portrait.
- Try different arrangements for your texts and visuals.
- Choose colours and fonts.
- Show your first draft to a few other students. Ask them to comment on the overall appearance.
- Ask one student to go over your work carefully, using the checklist on the activity sheet.
- Use the feedback to make adjustments.

Three sections of a personal profile

1. Write about your personality, your interests and what makes you unique.
   - Use the present tense.
   - Include a personal slogan or motto.

> **A personal slogan or motto** consists of a few words that describe you and your personality.
> Examples:
> *Tougher than the rest.*
> *Uniquely different.*
> *Strong but sensitive.*

- Also include a logo or symbol that represents you.

> **A logo or symbol** is a graphic representation that describes an aspect of your personality.
> Examples:

2. Write about an important event in your life that happened during this past school year.
   - Use the simple past tense and the past continuous.
3. Share your thoughts about your future and some of your concrete plans.
   - Use the future with *will* and *going to*.

- **Make the final version of your personal profile.**
  - Create your personal profile, taking the feedback from your classmates into account.
  - Revise and edit your texts carefully.
  - Make sure that the "real" you is evident.
  - If computers are available, use software to produce a polished product.
  - Ask yourself: Will this personal profile allow my classmates to know more about the "real" me?

3 POSTPRODUCTION

- **Present your personal profile to the class.**
  - Form a group of four.
  - Take turns presenting your personal profiles.
  - Comment on each other's profile.
  - Tell your classmates what information you found surprising.

- **Reflect on the project.**
  - Think back about what you learned in this unit and about the production process you used.

Media Alert

You are unique!
Make sure your profile is original and creative. Try new ideas, new colours ...
Dare to be different!

WOrd Wise

That's an unusual motto.
That logo is really you.
What does the logo represent?
I never knew that about you.
I like the design of your profile.

Annexes

Anthology

Summer Sensations

by Liam Patrick

Taste
the juicy **ripe** berries
dripping with the **dew**;
sweetened by the sun,
5 falling to a tender touch.

Hear
the soft songs of the **sparrow**
dancing in the trees;
a symphony of sounds
10 floating **'cross** the morning air.

Smell
the heady scent of roses
opening to the light;
the fragrance of the **firs**
15 drifting in the gentle **breeze**.

See
the first **blush** of the sun
rising **o'er** the hills
a humbling mix of **hues**
20 **dawning** in the azure sky.

Touch
the thick, spongy **moss**
climbing the rocky wall;
bask in the **balmy** air
25 **sheltering** my summer garden.

Grey Matter

by Margaret-Anne Colgan

I can hear my heart beat,
I can breathe in and out,
Frowning forehead,
Itchy toe,
5 I can move round about.

Nerve cells in the skull,
No one's quite the same;
Sneezing fit,
Winking eye,
10 All's possible with a brain.

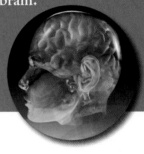

Glossary

ripe = ready to eat
dew = water droplets from night air
sweetened = made sweet, sugary
sparrow = small bird
'cross = across
firs = conifer trees
breeze = light wind
blush = turn red
o'er = over
hues = colours
dawning = beginning
moss = small, flowerless, green plants that
    grow in groups
bask = relax
balmy = peaceful
sheltering = protecting

frowning = looking angrily, grimacing
sneezing fit = to go 'achoo' many times
winking = closing one eye

Gus the Collie Hears a Family

by Naomi Lakritz

An **exuberant** border collie named Gus arrived in Winnipeg in February, 1984, to become Manitoba's first hearing ear dog.

Gus, one of seven hearing ear dogs in Canada, is trained to alert his deaf owners, Robert and Susan Zimmer, to the every day sounds that hearing people take for granted.

"He'll let them know when their baby's crying, the doorbell's ringing, and even when the teapot's boiling over," said Gus's trainer, Jacqueline Harbour, who runs Hearing Ear Dogs of Canada in Ancaster, Ont. She will spend about a week with the Zimmers helping Gus get adjusted to his new home and routine.

"I can hardly believe he's finally here. It's going to be wonderful," said an ecstatic Susan Zimmer. Both she and her husband have been deaf since childhood and tests have shown their seven-month old daughter, Laurie, is 90 per cent deaf.

"It's great because before we had to **keep track of** everything ourselves. We had flashing lights to warn us when the baby was crying. And once Robert forgot the bathwater was running and it nearly flooded the house because no one could hear it."

Gus responds to verbal commands as well as the hand signals his deaf masters use. He alerts them to household noises by leaping about or tapping them with his paw.

The dogs cost $2,000 but Gus was a gift to the Zimmers from the Imperial Order of Daughters of the Empire.

"We had bake sales, teas, you name it, to raise the money to bring Gus here. Now we're planning to get three more dogs to Manitoba families this fall," said IODE provincial president Pat Fowler.

Glossary
exuberant = excited
keep track of = check

Coloured Sounds

Adapted from Wendy Mass' novel
A MANGO-SHAPED SPACE

I

Freak. FREEEEEEK.

I'll never forget the first time I heard the word. I was eight. I was standing at the front of the class and the teacher was staring at me. She looked confused and more than a little **annoyed**. "What do you mean the right colours?"

"The colours of the numbers. Like the two is **cotton-candy** pink and the four is this baby-blanket blue colour… I figured it would be easier to do the math problem if I wrote the numbers in the right colours. Right?" My classmates started **giggling**. I felt my cheeks burning. Then I heard it. In a loud whisper from the back row. *Freak.* Except it sounded like *FREEEEK.*

"What are you talking about Mia?" demanded my now clearly **irate** teacher. "Numbers don't have colours, they simply have a shape and numerical value, that's all."

I stared at her. I suddenly felt very small. Of course numbers had colours. Were they also going to tell me that letters and sounds didn't have colours? That the letter *a* wasn't like a faded sunflower and chalk across the blackboard didn't make red **jagged** lines in the air? Was I the only one who lived in a world full of colour?

The teacher sent me to the principal's office. Later, sitting with my parents, I lied and said that I was only **fooling around**. I apologized. I never talked about it again, but I should have known. Big secrets like that are hard to keep forever. Everything is about to change. And there's nothing I can do to stop it.

❚❚

It's early in the school year and I've already failed two math quizzes. Failed with a bright-purple capital *F*. The note from my teacher is burning a hole in my pocket, and I know I should give it to my parents. I take a deep breath and walk into the living room where they are both sitting.

"I have to tell you guys something." Once the words are out, I am unable to make my lips work again.

They wait for me to continue. I take another deep breath.

"Remember in third grade when I told you that my numbers had colours?"

They think for a few seconds. "What about it?" my father asks.

"Well remember I told everyone I lied?"

"Vaguely," my mother continues. "What's this all about, Mia?"

"Well, the thing is," I begin, knowing there is no turning back now, "I wasn't lying. Numbers really *do* have colours for me. So do letters and sounds."

They are staring at me as if I just grew another head. But I keep talking.

"I used to think everyone saw these colours; then in third grade I realised it was just me. I thought I should tell you about it before I get two F's on my report card." I dig into my pocket and hand my mom the note. "You have to sign this."

I sit down on the armchair across from them, waiting for their reaction as they read the note together. I don't have to wait too long.

"Is this whole story some kind of joke to justify your difficulty with math?" asks my mother with a frown. "Because it wasn't funny in third grade and it isn't funny now."

"It isn't a joke, Mom," I reply, **gritting** my teeth.

My father studies me for a minute. "Do you mean to say you hallucinate?"

I shake my head. "It's not like that."

"*Hallucinating* means you imagine you see things that aren't there," my father adds.

I try not to lose my patience. "I know what the word means, Dad. But I'm not imagining things. My colours are as real as this house."

"What kinds of colours are these, exactly?" my mother asks. I can tell she's still not sure whether I'm lying.

I try to think of the easiest way to describe it. "Each letter and number has its own colour," I explain. "Like a *k* is turquoise blue, whether I think of it, read it, or hear it. It's just there, inside my head, plain as day."

Glossary
annoyed = irritated
cotton-candy = candied sugar
giggling = laughing lightly
irate = angry
jagged = uneven, irregular
fooling around = joking
gritting = tightly closing (teeth)

They continue to stare at me, and I begin to **squirm**.

"Sounds have colours too," I add. I want to tell them everything now. "**High-pitched** sounds give the sharpest colours. When I hear a noise, I'll see the colour and shape that go with —"

"Shape?" my father interrupts.

"Yes, shape," I say. "The colours appear in geometric shapes like spirals or balls or zigzags, that sort of thing. Or sometimes just a **hazy** patch of coloured air."

"Does this block your vision?" my mother asks hurriedly. "Does it hurt?"

I shake my head at both questions. "No, it's not really like that." My parents are looking at me strangely.

"I knew you'd think I'm crazy," I say, trying to keep my voice steady.

"We don't think you're crazy, Mia", my father says. "We just don't understand." He reaches over and takes my hands in his. "Do you remember when this started?"

"It's always been there," I tell him.

"Well," my father says, "we'll just have to call Dr Randolph. I'm sure he'll be able to help."

Over the years, Dr Randolph has cured us kids of everything from **chicken pox** to broken bones. He means well but he's getting old and a little forgetful. When my Dad finally does speak with him Dr Randolph recommends another doctor. His name is Dr Jerry Weiss.

III

My parents and I are sitting facing Dr Weiss in his office. Dr Randolph has called Dr Weiss and told him about my situation.

"And so what kind of medicine do you practice exactly, Dr Weiss?" my father asks, examining the many diplomas lining the walls.

"Please, call me Jerry." He continues, "As a neurologist, my focus is perception. I study how the brain processes information from our senses and how it sends that information back to the rest of the body. I've studied some unusual cases. Luckily, I'm one of the few researchers in the world who has experience with your condition."

My mother doesn't waste any time. "Can you tell us what's wrong with her?"

Jerry smiles gently. "There's nothing wrong with her."

"But something *is* wrong," I insist. "All the shapes and colours with the sounds and the letters and the numbers and —"

"Slow down," Jerry says, still smiling. "Mia, you don't have a disease. You don't even have a problem, exactly. What you have is a condition that is harmless. It's called synesthesia."

I stare at him for a minute trying to absorb what he just said. Somewhere in my head a chorus of voices sings *hallelujah*. There is a name for what I have! Even if it's difficult to pronounce it. "What do I have again?"

He says it again and I repeat it. It sounds like *sin-es-thee-ja*. He explains, "The word *synesthesia* means 'senses coming together.' Imagine that the wires in your brain are crossed, not literally of course. In your case, your visual and hearing senses are linked. The visual cortex in your brain is activated when your auditory cortex is stimulated."

"In *my* case?" I ask. "Do a lot of people have this?" I glance at my parents, who are clearly as surprised as I am.

Jerry shakes his head. "It's very uncommon. We now believe that everyone is born with it, but for most people the extra neural connections disappear. For one person in a couple of thousand, some of the connections stay. You see, the five senses can cross in many combinations. Seeing coloured letters and numbers – lexical synesthesia – is the most common form, followed by

coloured hearing. Like yourself, forty percent of synesthetes – that's the word for someone with synesthesia – have more than one type."

"How can we make it go away?" my mother asks. "Mia can't walk around seeing colours everywhere. It's interfering with her schoolwork."

"I understand your concerns, Mrs Winchell. Honestly, I do. But this is Mia's normal way of perceiving the world. She can learn to compensate for some things, but we can't 'cure' her. I've never met anyone who wanted their synesthesia to go away."

"I'm still in the room," I remind them.

"Mia," Jerry says, turning to me. "There are some things many synesthetes have in common, besides a slight majority of them being female. Why don't you tell me how many of them sound familiar to you, okay?"

I nod.

"Are you left-handed?"

"Yes."

"Are you artistic? Musical?"

"I paint. I don't play an instrument, but I listen to music a lot. I can always tell what note is being played by its colour. If a piano isn't tuned right, I can tell because the colours will be off."

"You're probably a very good speller, right?"

I nod again.

"Does everyone who has this synesthesia condition have all of these traits?" my mother asks, doubtfully.

"Not everyone, of course," Jerry says. "For instance, many people I've tested have problems with understanding math, but on the other hand, one of my former test subjects is now a college math professor. But it's **uncanny** how many characteristics they do share."

"It's certainly fascinating, Dr Weiss, er, Jerry," my father says. "But how can we help Mia?"

"Mia can train herself to make different mental connections by **narrowing** her focus and concentration. It will probably happen automatically as she gets older. Are you sure no one else in your family has this condition? It's often hereditary."

My parents shake their heads. "Will you work with her and see what you can do?" my mother asks.

"Of course," Jerry says. He tells us he has a class to teach now but invites me back the next day to do some tests.

"Are you going to **hook me up** to any wires?" I ask.

"No wires, I promise." Jerry walks us out to our car. I'm about to get in when he tells me to wait. He digs around his lab coat pockets and hands me a folded piece of paper. "Here's the address of a synesthesia web site where you can interact with people from all over the world."

I stare at the paper. "Other people with synesthesia?"

Jerry nods. "All kinds of people with all different types of synesthesia. There are discussion groups you can join and articles to read, although you might find some of them a bit dry."

I'm so excited that I give him a big hug. He waves good-bye as we pull out of the parking lot. I settle back in my seat, clutching the piece of paper Jerry gave me. I'm not crazy.

And the chorus belts out another round of *hallelujah*!

Glossary

squirm = twist and turn uncomfortably
high-pitched = acute, strident
hazy = cloudy
chicken pox = disease characterized by itchy red spots on the skin
uncanny = strange, mysterious
narrowing = reducing
hook up = connect, attach

The Most Mature Thing I've Ever Seen

by Chris Blake, Submitted by Leon Bunker
(from Chicken Soup for the Teenage Soul)

Every student at Monroe High School knew about it. Nobody did it. Nobody.

Lunch time at Monroe High was consistent. As soon as the bell that ended the last
5 morning class started ringing, the students **swarmed** toward their lockers. Then those who didn't eat in the cafeteria headed with their sack lunches toward the **quad**. The quad was a large, treeless square of concrete in the
10 center of campus. It was the meeting-and-eating place.

Around the quad the various school cliques assembled. The druggies lined up on the south side. The punkers were next to them. On the
15 east side were the brothers. Next to them were the nerds and brains. The **jocks** stood on the north side next to the surfers. The **rednecks** were on the west side. The socialites were in the cafeteria. Everybody knew their place.

20 This arrangement did create some tension. But for all the tension generated on the perimeter of the quad at lunchtime, it was nothing compared with the inside of the quad.

The inside was **no-man's land.**

25 Nobody at Monroe walked across the middle of the quad. To get from one side to the other, students walked around the quad. Around the people. Around the stares.

Everybody knew about it, so nobody did it.

30 Then one day at the beginning of spring, a new student arrived at Monroe. Her name was Lisa. She was unfamiliar to the area; in fact, she was new to the state.

And although Lisa was pleasant enough,
35 she did not quickly attract friends. She was **overweight** and shy, and the style of her clothes was not … right.

She had enrolled at Monroe that morning. All morning she had struggled to find her classes,
40 sometimes arriving late, which was especially embarrassing. The teachers had generally been tolerant, if not cordial. Some were irritated; their classes were already too large, and now this added paperwork before class.

45 But she had made it through the morning to lunch bell. Hearing the bell, she sighed and entered the crush of students in the hall. She weaved her way to her locker and tried her combination three, four, five times before it banged open.
50 Standing in front of her locker, she decided to carry along with her lunch all of her books for afternoon classes. She thought she could save herself another trip to her locker by eating lunch on the steps in front of her next class.

55 So Lisa began the longest walk of her life—the walk across campus toward her next class. Through the hall. Down the steps. Across the lawn. Across the sidewalk. Across the quad.

As Lisa walked she shifted the heavy books,
60 alternately resting the arm that held her light lunch. She had grabbed too many books; the top book kept slipping off, and she was forced to keep her eye on it in a balancing act as she moved past the people, shifting the books
65 from arm to arm, focusing on the balanced book, shuffling forward, oblivious to her surroundings.

All at once she sensed something: The air was eerily quiet. A nameless dread clutched her. She
70 stopped. She lifted her head.

Hundreds of eyes were staring. Cruel, hateful stares. Pitiless stares. Angry stares. Unfeeling, cold stares. They bore into her.

She froze, dazed, **pinned down**. Her mind
75 screamed, No! This can't be happening!

What happened next people couldn't say for
sure. Some later said she dropped her book,
reached down to pick it up, and lost her balance.
Some claimed she **tripped**. It didn't matter how
80 it happened.

She slipped to the pavement and lay there, legs
splayed, in the center of the quad.

Then the laughter started, like an electric
current jolting the perimeter, charged with a
85 **nightmarish** quality, wrapping itself around
and around its victim.

And she lay there.

From every side fingers pointed, and then the
taunt began, building in **raucous merriment**,
90 building in heartless **insanity**: "You! You! You!
YOU!"

Glossary

swarmed = moved in large numbers
quad = rectangular meeting area surrounded
     by buildings
jocks = athletes
rednecks = (offensive expression) white, rural,
     working class
no-man's land = an area of uncertainty and,
     often, danger
overweight = weighing too much; obese
pinned down = trapped
tripped = fell
splayed = inelegantly stretched out
nightmarish =   horrendous; like a very bad
     dream
taunt = jeers; insults
raucous = disorderly; rough
merriment = laughter
insanity = madness; craziness

And she lay there.

From the edge of the perimeter a figure emerged slowly. He was a tall boy, and he walked rigidly, as though he were measuring each step. He headed straight toward the place where the fingers pointed. As more and more students noticed someone else in the middle, the calls softened, and then they ceased. **A hush flickered over** the crowd.

The boy walked into the silence. He walked steadily, his eyes fixed on the form lying on the concrete.

By the time he reached the girl, the silence was deafening. The boy simply knelt and picked up the lunch sack and the scattered books, and then he placed his hand under the girl's arm and looked into her face. And she got up.

The boy steadied her once as they walked across the quad and through the quiet perimeter that parted before them.

The next day at Monroe High School at lunchtime a curious thing happened. As soon as the bell that ended the last morning class started ringing, the students swarmed toward their lockers. Then those who didn't eat in the cafeteria headed with their sack lunches across the quad.

From all parts of the campus, different groups of students walked freely across the quad. No one could really explain why it was okay now. Everybody just knew. And if you ever visit Monroe High School, that's how it is today.

It happened some time ago. I never even knew his name. But what he did, nobody who was there will ever forget.

Nobody.

GlOssary
a hush = a silence
flickered over = passed quickly over

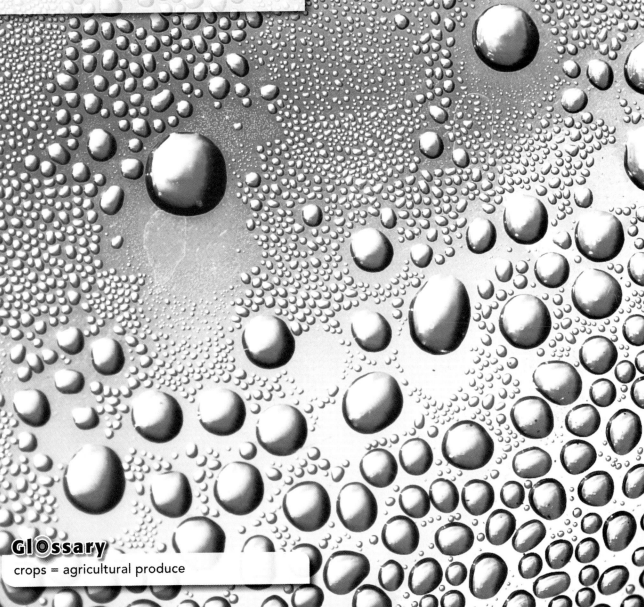

Rain

by Margaret-Anne Colgan

'How wonderful!' they cried,
'The rain has stopped for good;
The sun shall shine forever
Just like it always should!'

5 'How terrible!' they cried,
'The rain's no longer here;
The **crops** and food will burn out
And we will disappear!'

Glossary

crops = agricultural produce

The Little Dutch Boy

A Dutch folktale

*All people living in Holland have a great respect for the sea. After all, many Dutch people live on land that is below sea level. They are protected from the waters by **dikes** and barriers. The Dutch know that*
5 *the waters can flow in at any time and reclaim their land.*

This is a story about a brave little Dutch boy named Hans.

Once upon a time a young boy named Hans
10 lived happily with his mother and father in a small town by the sea. One lovely autumn afternoon Hans decided to visit his friend, Pieter, who lived at the other end of the dike. As Hans crossed the dike, he whistled to
15 himself. He was thankful for the warm sun for winter was approaching and the days were getting colder. When Hans reached the other side, he and Pieter played and laughed all afternoon. Finally evening fell and Hans
20 started on his walk home. It was later than he had thought and darkness was falling rapidly. He quickened his steps, thinking about the hot meal his mother was sure to have ready for him on his arrival.

25 It is a fact that when night falls things seem more hushed. This night on the dike near Haarlem it was no different. Hans could hear the wind whispering through the long grass of the fields on one side of the barrier. He could
30 hear the lapping of the water against the dike on the other side. Suddenly he heard a sound that was enough to freeze the blood of the bravest Dutch man. There, in the middle of the dike, Hans heard a **trickle** of water. Water
35 leaking through the dam would be disastrous for his town and the surrounding countryside. Hans looked around. With the help of the moonlight he saw a small hole in the dike;

water was slowly flowing through it. Hans
40 realised the danger immediately. If the water continued to flow through the trickle would become a stream and the water would finally break through the dike. What would become of his parents, his friends, his town? There was not
45 a moment to lose. Hans knew that he was too far away from the town to get help in time. He quickly climbed up the dike and jammed his finger into the hole. The water immediately stopped flowing. At first Hans was proud of his
50 quick thinking. "Nobody shall drown while I'm here," he thought, smiling to himself. "When I do not arrive home mother will realise something is wrong and send people out to search for me. They will find me soon." Hans was really quite
55 pleased with himself. But the minutes went by and turned into hours. His happiness gradually turned to dismay. Without the heat of the sun, the temperature began to drop. The wind that Hans had listened to earlier became colder and
60 Hans began to shiver. His finger slowly became **numb**. The numbness began to travel all over his body. "I cannot leave," Hans whispered to himself. "I cannot put my town in danger because I am a little cold. I am sure they will
65 find me soon," he consoled himself. He began to shout, "Help! Someone help me!" But nobody heard. The people of his town were **tucked** warmly **in** their houses. Silently, the midnight moon looked down at the **forlorn** boy.

70 Back at the house Hans' mother was quite upset at her son. When he had not come home for supper she presumed he had decided to stay the night at Jansen's house. She locked up the doors and made up her mind to talk to Hans the next
75 day. She did not like it when her son decided upon things without her permission.

Back on the dike Hans was trembling now. How could it be so cold at night? Hans knew he could not go home. The safety of his town depended on him. He might die here in the cold, but he would not sacrifice his family and friends for the warm bed he was dreaming about. He felt cold needles stabbing his arm and shoulder. He started to cry with the pain. At some time, sleep or unconsciousness claimed him. He forgot about the hot meal waiting for him. He forgot about his warm cozy bed. He forgot about his friends and family. He forgot about everything and surrendered to the cold night air.

The next morning, at the rising of the sun, an old man was out strolling by the fields near the dike. "Dawn," he reflected, "is the most beautiful time of the day." Suddenly his thoughts were interrupted by a groan. Where was it coming from? The old man looked around. He heard more groans. They seemed to be coming from the dike. He looked up and saw a young boy lying **shivering** against the wall of the water barrier. "My goodness," exclaimed the man, "what are you doing?"

Hans, who could barely talk because his **teeth were chattering** so much from the cold answered, "There is a small hole in the dike. I am keeping the water out so that the town does not flood." "Gracious!" cried the old man, "Let me get help," and he hurried to the town as fast as his legs could carry him. Soon help arrived for Hans: his parents, a doctor and men to fix the dike. "What a brave young man you are," declared the doctor as he gently placed Hans on a litter. "Your brave deed saved us all from a certain death." Hans smiled. His terrible night had not been in vain.

Glossary

dike = water barrier, dam
trickle = drop, drip
numb = frozen
tucked in = safe in bed
forlorn = sad
shivering = shaking with the cold
teeth were chattering = teeth were snapping together (from the cold)

Formal Date Dining

Adapted from pages 92 to 95 of
Emily Post's Teen Etiquette by
Elizabeth L. Post and Joan M. Coles

Going on a date to a formal restaurant can make even the most confident teen feel insecure. To prepare, let us imagine a formal date between Kevin and Caroline.

Kevin has finally decided to ask Caroline out on a date. He invites her to the Snooty Pig restaurant on Saturday night. It's a very special place and Caroline is very excited. She accepts Kevin's invitation.

Because the Snooty Pig is a popular restaurant, Kevin calls several days ahead to make a reservation. He tells the person taking the reservation what time he wants to eat and how many people will be with him. He mentions that it is a special occasion and requests a nice table.

When Kevin and Caroline arrive at the restaurant, Kevin lets Caroline out at the door and goes to park the car alone. Caroline waits for Kevin just inside the door and they go into the dining room together.

Once inside, Kevin leaves his coat at the coat check. He only leaves Caroline's coat if it is a **bulky** one. If she has an umbrella she should leave it with Kevin's coat. Kevin should remember that he has to tip the coat checker at the end of the evening. If Caroline is wearing a light coat she should wear it to the table. Once she is seated she can slip it off her shoulders.

If a headwaiter meets them at the door, Kevin gives his name and explains that they have reservations. The headwaiter will then lead the couple to their table. Kevin lets Caroline go first and follows behind her.

If the couple do not like the table they are given, perhaps because it is too near the kitchen, it is okay to ask for a better one. The head waiter gives Caroline the best seat at the table. He will hold the chair for her to sit.

Kevin waits for Caroline to be seated before he sits down. If the waiter gives them a banquette, Caroline waits for him to pull out the table and slides in first. If Kevin feels comfortable, he may help Caroline off with her coat.

When Caroline and Kevin are seated the waiter brings their menu. At this time they order beverages. They talk about what is on the menu. Caroline asks Kevin what food he is going to order. His answer tells her what his budget is. Caroline should order something that is similar in price to what Kevin is eating, unless Kevin says 'Order anything you like.'

In some really fancy restaurants, the woman's menu doesn't have any prices on it. In this case, Caroline should ask Kevin to help her make a selection. If she is too embarrassed to ask for help, she should order chicken or pasta because they are usually less expensive than steak or veal. Of course she can always choose to order the same thing as Kevin.

When the waiter comes with the menu, he may mention the chef's specials. These specials are not on the menu. The couple may ask the price of the specials if the waiter does not mention them. Kevin and Caroline may also ask him to describe any dishes they are not familiar with. If they are having trouble making up their minds, the couple may ask the waiter for his recommendations. They should never be too embarrassed to ask the waiter questions about the menu. After all, it's the waiter's job to answer questions about the food. It also makes his work more interesting.

MENUS

There are two types of menus – à la carte and *table d'hôte*. An à la carte menu lists each item with a price beside it. The cost of each item you order, including beverages, is added up to make your total bill. A *table d'hôte*, or "complete dinner", menu has a price beside the main course (often called the entrée). It then lists certain items – appetizers, soups, vegetables, salads, and desserts – with no prices. You may choose one item from each of these groups, unless the menu says otherwise, and the cost is included in the price of the entrée.

However, beware! There are almost always some items listed in these categories which do have prices beside them. If they do, the amount is charged in addition to the price of the main course. Many "complete dinner" menus will say "Price of entrée includes vegetable, potatoes, and dessert." That means the price of anything else – soup, salad, coffee – gets added to your bill.

Table d'hôte dinners are usually less expensive than the same items ordered one by one à la carte. Remember, though, you must stay within the limits of what the menu says or the cost goes up!

Glossary

bulky = big and difficult to manage

Love Letters

by Kate Walker

My name's Nick and my **chick's** name's Fleur. And she has a friend called Helen who's got a boyfriend named Clive. Now this Clive is really weird. Well, he does one weird thing I know of anyway: he writes three-page letters to his girlfriend, Helen, *every* day.

"What's wrong with the nerd" I asked Fleur. She'd spent a whole lunch time telling me about him.

"There's nothing *wrong* with him," she said. "You're so unromantic, Nick."

"Of course I'm not unromantic!" I said, and I offered her a lick of my ice cream to prove it. She groaned and pulled her P.E. bag over her head. She didn't want to talk to me anymore.

When girls go quiet, that's a bad sign!

"What's wrong?" I asked her.

"You don't love me," she said.

"Of course I love you," I told her. I offered her my whole ice cream. She wouldn't take it.

"You don't love me *enough*," she said.

"How much is *enough*?"

How much ice cream did it take?

"You don't write me letters like Clive does to Helen," she said.

"I don't need to, I see you every day in Computers," I said. "*And* Chemistry."

"Clive sees Helen every day in Biology, and Textiles, and Home Science, and assembly, and roll call," she said, "and he writes letters to *her*!"

I knew what was happening here: my girlfriend was **cooling on me**.

"OK," I said, "I'll write you a letter."

"Aw, Nick!" She whipped her P.E. bag off her head.

I was glad I'd weakened. Fleur is really gorgeous. I couldn't risk losing her for the sake of a few lines scrawled on a piece of paper. I'm the envy of the boys' locker room, having her for a girlfriend.

I sat down that night and began my first letter: "Dear Fleur…" Then I stared at the page for the next half hour. What do you write in letters to someone you see every day? I chewed my pencil; I chewed my nails. Then, in desperation, I finally asked Mum.

"Write about the things you have in common," Mum said, so I wrote the following: "Wasn't that computer class on Tuesday a ROAR? The best bit was when Brando tilted the computer to show us the little button underneath and the monitor fell off."

I wrote about the Chemistry class too, though it wasn't quite as interesting. Not a single kid muffed their experiment and blew their eyebrows off. But then I got really creative at the end of the letter and added a postscript written in Basic.

I got the letter back next day with "five-and-a-half out of twenty" marked on the bottom.

"What was wrong with it?" I asked Fleur.

"You made a lot of spelling mistakes for one thing," she said.

"I was being *myself*!" I told her.

"I didn't notice," she said. "you didn't say anything *personal* in it!"

Is that what she wanted, a *personal* letter?

I thought it over for five minutes. There were guys all round the lunch area just waiting to take my place and share their chocolate milk with the fabulous Fleur. If revealing a few personal secrets was what it took to keep her, I could do it.

"Dear Fleur…" I began the second letter that night. "This is not something I'd tell everyone, but I use a deodorant. Only on sports days or in really hot weather of course."

No, that was too personal. I ripped up the page and started again. "Dear Fleur, Guess what? Mrs. Hessel blew me up in History today for no reason at all. I was embarrassed to death. Goggle-eyes Gilda laughed her stupid head off."

Actually, once I'd got started I found the personal stuff not that hard to write. I told Fleur what mark I'd *really* got in the English half-yearlies. Then I told her about a movie I'd seen where this pioneer farming guy loses his plow horse, then loses his wife, then his children, and then his cows get hoof rot. But even though he sits down and **bawls** his eyes out about it, in the end he walks off into the sunset, a stronger man.

"I'd like to suffer a great personal loss like that," I told Fleur in the letter, "and walk away stronger and nobler for it."

Her sole comment on letter number two was: "You didn't say anything in it about *me*." And she went off to eat lunch with Helen.

It was time to hit the panic button. Fleur was "**drifting**." I stuffed my sandwiches back in my bag and went looking for Clive. I bailed him up under the stairwell.

"OK, what do you put in your letters to Helen?" I asked him.

Clive turned out to be a decent kid. He not only told me, he gave me a photocopy of the latest letter he was writing to Helen.

You should have seen it!

"Darling Helen, Your hair is like gold. Your eyes remind me of **twilight** reflected on Throsby Creek. Your ear lobes are… Your eyelashes are…" And so on. It was what you'd call a poetic autopsy.

And as if that wasn't bad enough, he then got into the declarations of love: "You're special to me because… I yearn for you in History because… I can't eat noodles without thinking of you because…"

"Do girls really go for this sort of thing?" I asked him.

"Helen does," he said. "She'd drop me tomorrow if I stopped writing her letters. It's the price you pay if you want to keep your girlfriend."

So I began my third letter, with Clive's photocopy propped up in front of me as a guide.

"Dear Fleur, Your hair is like…" I began.

Actually, I'd always thought it was like cotton candy, pretty from a distance but all **gooey** when you touched it – too much hair spray, I suppose.

I scrapped that opening and started again.

"Dear Fleur, Your eyes are like…"

Actually, they're a bit small and **squinty**. I think she might need glasses but she's not **letting on**.

Scrub the eyes.

"Dear Fleur, Your face is excellent overall. You look like one of those soap-opera dolls."

I thought I would've been able to go on for hours about her face, but having said that, it seemed to sum her up.

I moved on to the declarations: "I love you because…" I chewed my pencil again, then my fingernails. This time I couldn't ask Mum.

Why did I love Fleur? Because she was **spunky**. Because all the guys thought so too. Well, not all of them. Some of them thought she wasn't all that interesting to talk to, but I put that down to jealousy.

Still, I began to wonder, what *had* we talked about in the three weeks we'd been going together? Not much really. She'd never been interested enough in my hockey playing to ask in-depth questions about it. And, I have to admit, I hadn't found her conversation on white ankle boots all that **riveting** either.

No wonder I was having so much trouble writing letters to her. We had nothing in c ommon. I barely knew her. What were her views on nuclear disarmament? Maybe she didn't have any. Was she pro-Libyan? I didn't know.

I scrapped the letter, scrapped Clive's photocopy, and started again, this time with no trouble at all.

"Dear Fleur, This writing of letters was a very good idea because it gives me the opportunity to say something important to you. I think you're a nice girl and I've enjoyed going steady with you for three weeks but I think we should call it off. Even if it's a great personal loss to both of us, I'm sure we'll walk away stronger and nobler. Yours sincerely, Nick."

I slipped the letter to her in Computers. She didn't take it too badly, just ripped it up and fed it through the shredder. But then two days later photocopies of my *personal* letter started to circulate the school.

I didn't mind, though, because as a result of that, Goggle-eyes Gilda slipped me a note in History that said, briefly: "I like your style, Nick. You've got depth." I took another look at Goggle-eyes. I didn't mind her style either. She has this terrific laugh and she's a **whiz** on computers.

I wrote back straightaway, my own kind of letter this time—honest and to the point: "Dear Gilda, That three-minute talk you gave on speech day about Third World Famine Relief was really excellent. I'll be eating lunch in the quad if you'd care to join me."

Gl**O**ssary

chick = girl
cooling on me = losing interest in me
bawls = cries loudly
drifting = slowly moving away
twilight = nightfall
gooey = soft and sticky
squinty = narrow
letting on = admitting
scrub = eliminate
spunky = has a strong character
riveting = interesting
whiz = smart person

The Pirate Don Durk of Dowdee

by Mildred Plew Meigs

Ho, for the Pirate Don Durk of Dowdee!
He was as wicked as wicked could be,
But oh, he was perfectly gorgeous to see!
    The Pirate Don Durk of Dowdee.

5 His conscience, of course, was as black as a bat,
But he had a **floppety** plume on his hat
And when he went walking it jiggled—like that!
    The plume of the Pirate Dowdee.

His coat it was crimson and cut with a slash,
10 And often as ever he **twirled** his mustache.
Deep down in the ocean the mermaids went splash,
    Because of Don Durk of Dowdee.

Moreover, Dowdee had a purple tattoo,
And stuck in his belt where he buckled it through
15 Were a **dagger**, a **dirk** and a **squizzamaroo**,
    For fierce was the Pirate Dowdee.

So fearful he was he would shoot at a **puff**,
And always at sea when the weather grew rough
He drank from a bottle and wrote on his **cuff**,
20   Did Pirate Don Durk of Dowdee.

Oh, he had a **cutlass** that swung at his thigh
And he had a parrot called Pepperkin Pye,
And a zigzaggy scar at the end of his eye
    Had Pirate Don Durk of Dowdee.

25 He kept in a cavern, this **buccaneer** bold,
A curious chest that was covered with **mould**,
And all of his pockets were jingly with gold!
    Oh jing! went the gold of Dowdee.

His conscience, of course, it was crook'd like **a squash**,
30 But both of his boots made a **slickery slosh**,
And he went through the world with a wonderful **swash**,
    Did Pirate Don Durk of Dowdee.

It's true he was wicked as wicked could be,
His sins they outnumbered a hundred and three,
35 But oh, he was perfectly gorgeous to see,
    The Pirate Don Durk of Dowdee.

Glossary

floppety = drooping, hanging
twirled = twisted
dagger = knife
dirk = long knife
squizzamaroo = a pistol
puff = cloud
cuff = end of a sleeve
cutlass = sword
buccaneer = pirate
mould = fungus
a squash = orange or yellow fruit eaten
   like a vegetable
slickery = polished, smooth
slosh = splash
swash = arrogant walk

Sing a Song of Sixpence

An English Nursery Rhyme

Sing a song of sixpence
A pocket full of **rye**
Four and twenty blackbirds
Baked in a pie

5 When the pie was opened
The birds began to sing
Was that not a **dainty** dish
To set before a king?

The King was in his counting house
10 Counting out his money
The Queen was in the parlor
Eating bread and honey

The Maid was in the garden
Hanging out the clothes
15 When down came a blackbird
And snapped off her nose!

Sky Dancers

by Connie Anne Kirk

Holding the trunk, John Cloud felt the rough bark against his cheek as he stood in the tree. Right foot, pull. Left foot, pull. Again he had climbed as far as he
5 dared, yet there was still a long way to go. He tested one foot up on the third branch and pressed some weight on it. The branch bobbed up and down, waving its leaves at no one in particular. No. Not yet.

10 John Cloud leaned back against the tree trunk and felt its strength and wisdom. It was an old tree that had held many moons between its branches. The tree and Mother Earth and Father Sky would let him know
15 when it was time to go higher.

Glossary
rye = grain cereal
dainty = special

I Am...

by Amy Yerkes

I am an architect: I've built a solid foundation; and each year I go to that school I add another floor of wisdom and knowledge.

I am a sculptor: I've shaped my morals and philosophies according to the clay of right and wrong.

I am a painter: With each new idea I express, I paint a new **hue** in the world's multitude of colors.

I am a scientist: Each day that passes by, I gather new data, make important observations, and experiment with new concepts and ideas.

I am an astrologist: reading and analyzing the palms of life and each new person I encounter.

I am an astronaut: constantly exploring and broadening my horizons.

I am a doctor: I heal those who turn to me for consultation and advice, and I bring out the vitality in those who seem lifeless.

I am a lawyer: I'm not afraid to stand up for the inevitable and basic rights of myself and all others.

I am a police officer: I always watch out for others' welfare and I am always on the scene preventing fights and keeping the peace.

I am a teacher: By my example others learn the importance of determination, dedication and hard work.

I am a mathematician: making sure I conquer each one of my problems with correct solutions.

I am a detective: peering through my two lenses, searching for meaning and significance in the mysteries of life.

I am a jury member: judging others and their situations only after I've heard and understood the entire story.

I am a banker: Others share their trust and values with me and never lose interest.

I am a hockey player: watching out for and **dodging** those who try to block my goal.

I am a marathon runner: full of energy, always moving and ready for the next challenge.

I am a mountain climber: Slowly but surely I am making my way to the top.

I am a tight-rope walker: Carefully and **stealthily** I pace myself through every rough time, but I always make it safely to the end.

I am a millionaire: rich in love, sincerity and compassion, and I own a wealth of knowledge, wisdom, experience and **insight** that is priceless.

Most important, I am me.

Glossary

hue = colour, shade
dodging = avoiding, keeping away from
stealthily = cautiously
insight = intuition

A Simple Gesture

by John W. Schlatter

Everybody can be great ... because anybody can serve. You don't have to have a college degree to serve. You don't have to make your subject and verb agree to serve. You only need a heart full of grace. A soul generated by love.

Martin Luther King, Jr.

Mark was walking home from school one day when he noticed the boy ahead of him had tripped and dropped all of the books he was carrying, along with two sweaters, a baseball bat, a glove and a small tape recorder. Mark knelt down and helped the boy pick up the scattered articles. Since they were going the same way, he helped to carry part of the **burden**. As they walked Mark discovered the boy's name was Bill, that he loved video games, baseball and history, that he was having a lot of trouble with his other subjects and that he had just broken up with his girlfriend.

They arrived at Bill's home first and Mark was invited in for a cola and to watch some television. The afternoon passed pleasantly with a few laughs and some shared small talk, then Mark went home. They continued to see each other around school, had lunch together once or twice, then both graduated from junior high school. They ended up in the same high school where they had brief contacts over the years. Finally the long awaited senior year came, and three weeks before graduation, Bill asked Mark if they could talk.

Bill reminded him of the day years ago when they had first met. "Do you ever wonder why I was carrying so many things home that day?" asked Bill. "You see, I cleaned out my locker because I had decided not to go home. I had saved up enough money and was going to leave town and start over somewhere else. But after we spent some time together talking and laughing, I realized that if I had gone, I would have missed that time and so many others that might follow. So you see, Mark, when you picked up my books that day, you did a lot more. You saved me."

Gl☉ssary
burden = heavy load, heavy weight

A Letter from the Fringe

Adapted from a story by Joan Bauer

This is dedicated to every kid who has ever been called a hurtful name. And to every kid who has tried to feel superior by putting down someone else.

Today they got Sally.

She wasn't doing anything. Just eating a cookie that her aunt had made for her. We were sitting at the fringe table in the back of the lunchroom. The fringe table is as far away from the in-crowd table as you can get and still be in the cafeteria.

I saw Doug Booker before she did. Saw his eyes get that hard glint they always get right before he says something **mean**. Watched him walk toward us. He was joined by Charlie Bass, who was smirking and laughing and looking at Sally as if the sight of her hurt his eyes.

I swallowed the cookie Sally had given me. Felt my stomach tense. It was too late to grab Sally and walk off.

'In-crowders at four o'clock,' I warned her.

Sally looked up to **smirks**. Her face went pale.

Booker started. 'So, *Sals,* maybe you should be cutting back on those calories, huh?'

Charlie was laughing away.

'What have you got, Sals, about thirty pounds to lose? More?' He did a *tsk, tsk.* Looked her up and down with disgust.

All she could do was look down.

I stood up. 'Get lost, Booker.'

Sneer. Snort. 'Now how can I get lost in a school?'

'Booker, I think you have the innate ability to get lost just about anywhere.'

'Why don't you and your fat friend just get out of my face because the two of you are so ugly you're making me sick and I don't know if I can hold the puke in!'

He and Charlie **strolled off**.

There is no response to that kind of hate.

I looked at Sally who was gripping her cookie bag.

I tried fighting through the words like my mom and dad had taught me. Taking each one apart like I'm diffusing a bomb.

Was Sally fat?

I sucked in my stomach. She needed to lose some weight, but who doesn't.

Were she and I so disgusting we could make someone sick?

We're not Hollywood beauties, but who is?

If Booker said we were serial killers, we could have laughed it off. But gifted bullies use partial truths. Doug knew how to get personal.

I didn't know what to say. 'They're total **creeps**, Sally.'

She sat there broken, holding her cookie bag that I just noticed had pictures of balloons on it.

'It's my birthday,' she said quietly.

'Oh, Sally, I didn't know that.'

She looked up. 'I just want to ignore those people,' she said sadly.

'Can you do it though?' I asked her.

She shrugged, mumbled, and looked down again.

It's hard. For me, sure, I can pretend I'm ignoring something or someone mean, but it doesn't help if deep down I'm angry, and as I push it farther down, the anger gets hotter.

So the biggest thing that's helped me **cope** is that I've stopped hoping that the mean in-crowders get punished for their cruelty. I think in some ways they have their punishments already. As my mom says, meanness never just goes out of a person – it goes back to them as well.

I remember once when Parker Cravens, an in-crowder, and I had to be lab partners. She looked at me like I was a dead frog she had to dissect. Parker's family is rich. As a result she thinks anyone who is not wealthy is below her. At first I was annoyed at the way she treated me, then I started looking at her under the emotional microscope.

'Parker, do you like this class?' I asked.

She glanced at the sports watch that I'd bought for two bucks at a flea market and shuddered. 'My dad's making me take it. He's a doctor and he said I've got to know this stuff.'

'What class would you rather take?'

She looked at me as if my question was totally stupid.

'No, really. Parker, which one?'

'Art history,' she said.

'Why don't you take it?'

Quiet voice. 'My dad won't let me.'

'Why not?'

'He wants me to be a doctor.'

Parker would last two nanoseconds in medical school.

'That's got to be hard,' I offered.

'Like granite, Dana.'

It's funny. No matter how mean she gets – and Parker can get mean – every time I see her now, I don't just think that she's the prettiest girl in the school or the richest or the most popular; I think a little about how her father doesn't have a clue as to what she wants to be, and how much that must **hurt**.

My bedroom doesn't look like I feel. It's yellow and sunny. It's got posters of Albert Einstein and Eleanor Roosevelt and their best quotes.

Al's: *If at first the idea is not absurd, then there is no hope for it.*

Eleanor's: *No one can make you feel inferior without your consent.*

I flop on the bed wondering how come cruelty seems so easy for some people. It's strange: you can never be too athletic, too popular, too gorgeous, or too rich, but you can be too smart and too nerdy.

My mom tells me that sometimes people try to control others when too many things are out of control in their own lives.

I hug my bear Quantas. He has always been my best confidante, ever since I was four years old. And it's funny. As I hold him now, all kinds of things seem possible.

Like the Letter. I've been tossing the idea around for a long time: how I could write a letter to the in-crowders, explain what life is like from my end of the lunchroom, and maybe things would get better at my school.

I look at Quantas. 'If I had the guts to write a letter to the in-crowd at my school, this is what I'd like to say:

'This letter could be from the nerd with the thick glasses in the computer lab. It could be from the '**zit** girl' who won't look people in the eye because she's embarrassed about her skin. It could be from the guy with the nose ring who you call queer, or any of the kids you don't like for whatever reason.

'You know, I've got things inside me – dreams and nightmares, plans and mess-ups. In that regard, we have things in common. But we never seem to connect through those common experiences because I'm so different from you.

'My being different doesn't mean that you're better than me. I think you've always assumed that I want to be like you. But I want you to know something about kids like me. We just want the freedom to walk down the hall without seeing your smirks, your contempt, and your looks of disgust.

'Sometimes I stand far away from you in the hall and watch what you do to other people. I wonder why you've chosen to make the world a worse place.

Glossary

mean = unkind
smirks = unkind smiles
strolled off = walked away nonchalantly
creeps = unpleasant people
cope = manage, continue on
hurt = feel bad
zit = pimple, blackhead

'I wonder, too, what really drives the whole thing. Is it hate? Is it power? Are you afraid if you get too close to me and my friends
155 that some of our uncoolness will rub off on you? I think what could really happen is that learning tolerance could make us happier, freer people.

'What's it going to be like when we all get
160 older? Will we be more tolerant, or less because we haven't practiced it much? I think of the butterflies in the science museum. There are hundreds of them in cases. Hundreds of different kinds. If they were all the same, it
165 would be so boring. You can't look at the blue ones or the striped ones and say they shouldn't have been born. It seems like nature is trying to tell us something. Some trees are tall, some are short. Some places have mountains, others have
170 deserts. Some cities are always warm, some have different seasons. Flowers are different. Animals. Why do human beings think they have the right to pick who's best – who's acceptable and who's not?

175 'I used to give you control over my emotions. I figured that if you said I was gross and weird, it must be true. How you choose to respond to people is up to you, but I won't let you be my judge and jury. I'm going to remind you
180 every chance I get that I have as much right to be on this earth as you.'

I look at Quantas. Then, I turn on my computer and begin to write it all down finally. The words just pour out, but I know
185 the letter isn't for the in-crowders.

It's for me.

And one other person.

I open my desk drawer where I keep my stash of emergency birthday cards. I pick one that
190 reads: *It's your birthday. If you'd reminded me sooner, this card wouldn't be late.*

I sign the card; print the letter out, fold it in four so that it will fit inside, and write Sally's name on the envelope.

Magic Video

by Jeff Siamon

The teenagers, Frankie, John, Nabeel, and Abbi are employees at the video store. John really likes Abbi and would like to ask her out, but he is too shy to do so. As Scene 3 opens, Nabeel is trying to
5 *push John into telling Abbi that he likes her.*

Scene 3: Video Store

Nabeel takes John to one side. Frankie and Abbi continue chatting at the counter, while Abbi waits on customers.

10 Nabeel: So are you going to tell her tonight?

John: No.

Nabeel: You're **chickening out** on me, John.

John: I'm not chickening out, I'm just…I just don't want to tell her. At least not
15 now. Maybe another night. Maybe tomorrow night.

Nabeel: Maybe never. Hey, buddy, how long are you going to torture yourself like this? You like her. You work with her alone
20 two nights a week. At least tell her. What have you got to lose?

John: Nothing, but…

Nabeel: Aren't I a friend? Aren't I trying to help you?

25 John: Yeah, but, I'm no good with words around her. All I can do is stammer.

Nabeel: Here, try this. This will work (*He hands John a piece of paper.*)

John: Not another one of your brilliant
30 suggestions. (*reading*) "Lookit babe, why don't we become an item?" An item? I'm not going to say this.

Nabeel: Trust me. It'll work.

John: People don't talk like this.

35	Nabeel:	They do if they're trying to impress somebody.
	John:	Forget it. (*handing back the paper*) Thanks, but…
40	Nabeel:	No, keep it. Maybe you'll change your mind.
	John:	Maybe I'll win the lottery, but I'll be too old to care.
	Nabeel:	Well, man, it's your love life. I'm only trying to help.
45	John:	Yeah, well, thanks. Anyway, I have a plan. I just have to get up the nerve to use it. I saw it once in a movie.
	Nabeel:	Oh, yeah? That doesn't sound good. What is it?
50	John:	Well, I'd send her this anonymous note…
	Nabeel:	Come on, John, you've seen too many movies.
	John:	No, wait. I'd send her this anonymous note telling her how I feel. "Dear Abbi…"
55	Nabeel:	Hey, you're not asking for advice, you know.
	John:	Okay. "To whom it may concern."
	Nabeel:	Very romantic. How about "To the special lady in my life"?
60	John:	No. She's not really old enough to be a lady.
	Nabeel:	Okay, then, "To the special girl in my life." Better still, "To the most beautiful girl in my life."
65	John:	Are you kidding? She'd hate that sexist line. She's not going to respect any guy who calls her beautiful.
	Nabeel:	All right, "To the ugliest girl in my life."
	John:	Would you just let me finish?
70	Nabeel:	I don't think you're ever going to get past the introduction.
	John:	Dear *Ms.* Abbi.
	Nabeel:	Ms.?

	John:	Nabeel, smother it in onions and put it out for the garbage. I listen to your ideas. Now listen to mine.
	Nabeel:	Okay. How about, "Dear babe"?
	John:	"Dear babe"? Whatever. "Dear babe, you don't know me, but I see you every day in school."
80	Nabeel:	Good beginning.
	John:	"I'd like to get to know you better, but I guess I'm too shy to talk to you."
	Nabeel:	Good. That's good.
85	John:	Um…"I'm too shy to talk to you. If you're interested in finding out who I am, meet me tonight at Pizza Palace. I'll be wearing dark glasses, and I'll be looking for only you."
90	Nabeel:	Hey, that's good.
	John:	Do you really think so?
	Nabeel:	Man, I think you've got potential.
	John:	Yeah, well, it's an idea, anyway.
	Nabeel:	A good idea. So do it.
95	John:	No, it probably wouldn't work.
	Nabeel:	Try it. It's simple. It's direct. It's great.
	John:	I don't know.
	Nabeel:	John, you're never going to tell her. And one of these days it's going to be too late.
100	John:	I'll tell her. Someday, I'll tell her. I will.

John and Nabeel begin to move across the stage toward Abbi and Frankie.

	Nabeel:	Hidden potential. Very hidden. (*to Frankie*) Come on, Frankie, let's go.
105		Our limo awaits us.
	Frankie:	You're weird. Bye, Abbi. Bye, John.
	Abbi:	Bye.
	John:	Bye.

Glossary

chickening out = becoming scared

From Writing in Context Three Grade 9 Text by GRAVES CLAYTON. 1992. Reprinted with permission of Nelson, a division of Thomson Learning: www.thomsonrights.com. Fax 800 730-2215

Vocabulary in Context

A

able (*adjective*) capable

ahead (*adverb*) in front of you, that is about to start

almost (*adverb*) very nearly, practically

alone (*adjective*) the only one

ask someone out (*phrasal verb*) invite someone on a date

asleep (*adjective*) sleeping, not awake

avoid (*verb*) prevent, stay away from

awake (*adjective*) not asleep

B

baked (*adjective*) cooked in the oven

beat (*noun*) rhythm, cadence

binder (*noun*) folder that holds loose sheets of paper together

blind (*adjective*) unable to see

blood (*noun*) red liquid that circulates through the body

blood vessels (*compound noun, plural*) tubes in the body (arteries, veins and capillaries) through which blood circulates

brain (*noun*) organ inside the head that controls thoughts, emotions, bodily functions and movement

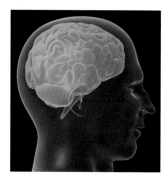

C

chickpea (*noun*) round, yellow legume cooked and served as a vegetable

cough (*noun, verb*) expulsion of air out of the mouth with a loud noise, usually because of a cold or smoke

D

darkness (*noun*) absence of light

deprivation (*noun*) insufficient amount of

distracted (*adjective*) confused, inattentive

E

effective (*adjective*) producing the desired result

elderly (*adjective*) old

energized (*adjective*) full of energy

enjoy (*verb*) get pleasure from

enough (*adjective*) sufficient quantities of

especially (*adverb*) particularly

exhausted (*adjective*) very tired

F

fight (*verb*) combat

food for thought (*expression*) something you should think about

forget (*verb*) not remember

frozen (*adjective*) immobile

G

get hold of (*phrasal verb*) capture, take

grab (*verb*) take suddenly

grades (*noun, plural*) school results

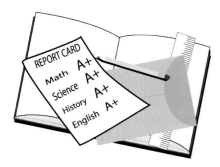

H

habit (*noun*) something a person does regularly

headache (*noun*) pain in your head

health (*noun*) condition of a person's body or mind

hope (*verb*) want something to happen or be true

hug (*noun*) putting your arms around something or someone to give affection

hungry (*adjective*) in need of food

hurry (*verb*) go quickly

I

immune system (*compound noun*) system in the body that fights infections

improve (*verb*) make better

be **into** something (*phrasal verb*) be very interested in something

involved (*adjective*) taking part in

K

keep up with (*phrasal verb*) stay up to date with

knowledge (*noun*) the information retained by your mind

L

laugh (*verb*) make sounds that show you are happy or amused

laughter (*noun*) act or sound of laughing

at least (*adverb*) a minimum of, not less than

level (*noun*) amount, size or number of something

limbic system (*compound noun*) system in the brain that controls emotions, feelings and sensations

loud and clear (*expression*) very clearly, well

lower (*verb*) reduce

lung (*noun*) organ in the body used for breathing

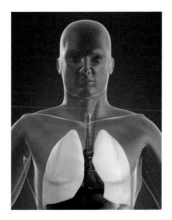

M

management (*noun*) control, organization

maybe (*adverb*) possibly

(M continued)

memories (*noun, plural*) moments you remember from the past

memory (*noun*) ability to remember

midnight (*noun*) twelve o'clock at night

mind (*noun*) part of the brain that controls and generates thoughts

miss (*verb*) not see, not watch

multi-tasking (*adjective*) doing more than one thing at a time

N

notice (*verb*) see and be aware of

O

olfactory (*adjective*) relating to the sense of smell

once (*adverb*) one time

oversleep (*verb*) to sleep in late or sleep too much

own (*adjective*) belonging to you

P

palate (*noun*) top part of the inside of the mouth

pay attention (*verb*) concentrate

perceive (*verb*) notice

physical rehabilitation (*compound noun*) training and exercise to repair the body

poll (*noun*) survey to compile statistics

powerful (*adjective*) strong

prevent (*verb*) stop

prove yourself (*phrasal verb*) show what you can do

pull up (*phrasal verb*) stop a vehicle,

punish (*verb*) make (someone) pay a penalty for bad behaviour

R

reach for (*phrasal verb*) take

recall (*verb*) remember

relief (*noun*) deliverance from something unpleasant

rely on (*phrasal verb*) depend on

remind (*verb*) cause to remember

right (*adjective*) correct

rules (*noun, plural*) official instructions for a game, what you can and cannot do

rush (*verb*) do something very quickly

S

scent (*noun*) odour

secondhand smoke (*compound noun*) smoke you breathe in from another person's cigarette

shovel (*verb*) remove snow

show off (*phrasal verb*) demonstrate

sight (*noun*) ability to see

sighted (*adjective*) who can see

skin (*noun*) natural outer cover of the body

slip (*verb*) loose your balance

smell (*noun*) ability to identify something by using the nose

sneeze (*noun*) sudden explusion of air from the nose and mouth usually because of a cold or irritation

state of mind (*compound noun*) how somebody feels emotionally

stressed out (*compound adjective*) tired, anxious because of stress

stressful (*adjective*) causing stress

such as (*noun*) for example

swallow (*verb*) make food or drink pass down the throat

swollen (*adjective*) enlarged, filled with excess blood

T

taste (*noun*) ability to recognize flavour of food or drink

taste bud (*compound noun*) sensory organs on surface of tongue

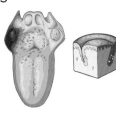

teen, teenager (*noun*) person between 13 and 19 years old

tip (*noun*) piece of useful advice

tray (*noun*) platter

treat (*noun*) something that is very enjoyable

turn out to be (*phrasal verb*) prove to be, end up being

twice (*adverb*) two times

U

uneasy (*adjective*) uncomfortable

unfortunately (*adverb*) unluckily

until (*preposition*) up to the time when

usually (*adverb*) normally

V

volunteer (*verb*) work without pay

W

warm (*adjective*) temperature between cool and hot

wealthy (*adjective*) having lots of money

well-being (*compound noun*) feeling of being healthy and happy

wise (*adjective*) having good judgment

wrong (*adjective*) not correct

A

above (*preposition*) over

advertised (*adjective*) promoted, publicized

ago (*adverb*) in the past

almost (*adverb*) nearly

among (*preposition*) in the company of, with

amount (*noun*) quantity

ankle (*noun*) bone connecting the foot to the leg

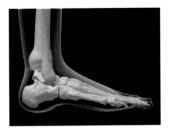

available (*adjective*) obtainable, accessible

average (*adjective*) normal, usual

become **aware** of (*phrasal verb*) recognize, notice

B

believe (*verb*) think, suppose

bell-bottomed (*adjective*) become wider at the bottom

below (*preposition*) under

both (*adjective*) the two

brand name (*compound noun*) name of company that makes a product

broadcast (*verb*) transmit by radio or television

build (*verb*) construct

C

care about (*phrasal verb*) be concerned with, interested in

chemicals (*noun, plural*) artificial substances produced through chemistry

coal (*noun*) black mineral burned to give heat

make a **comeback** (*expression*) become fashionable again

crew (*noun*) team

D

decade (*noun*) period of ten years

den (*noun*) underground home or cave of some animals

drought (*noun*) long period of time when there is no rain

E

emit (*verb*) send out, discharge

enjoy (*verb*) take pleasure from, like

environmentally friendly (*compound adjective*) good for the environment

escape (*verb*) get away, free

F

fade out (*phrasal verb*) slowly disappear

fine (*noun*) sum of money in payment for an offence

flooding (*noun*) inundation

fortunately (*adverb*) luckily

G

get around (*phrasal verb*) travel

groundhog (*noun*) marmot

grow (*verb*) get bigger

H

on the other **hand** (*expression*) from another point of view

hang out with (*phrasal verb*) spend time with

harmful (*adjective*) dangerous

heel (*noun*) back part of foot or shoe

hiking (*noun*) long walk in the countryside or mountains

household (*noun*) group of people who live in one house

I

increase (*verb*) augment

inexpensive (*adjective*) not costing very much

J

jitterbug (*noun*) fast American dance popular in the 1940s

K

keep (*verb*) conserve

keep in mind (*phrasal verb*) remember

kind (*noun*) type

L

last (*verb*) continue

be on the **lookout** for (*expression*) pay attention to

M

made up of (*compound adjective*) composed of

many (*adjective*) a large quantity of

mall (*noun*) shopping centre

melt (*verb*) become liquid

mind (*noun*) part of brain that thinks and remembers

on the **move** (*expression*) in motion, travelling

N

news (*noun*) information about a recent event

notice (*verb*) observe

O

own (*adjective*) belonging to you

P

pastime (*noun*) hobby

peace (*noun*) absence of war

platform shoes (*compound noun*) shoes with thick soles and high heels

power (*verb*) supply energy to

powerful (*adjective*) efficient

previous (*adjective*) the one before

provide (*verb*) give, supply

R

ray (*noun*) line of light or radiation from the sun

reach (*verb*) attain, become

release (*verb*) *generate, produce*

rise (*noun*) increase

S

screen (*noun*) glass surface of computer or TV

seam (*noun*) line where two pieces of material are joined

shadow (*noun*) dark area produced by blocking the light

sideburns (*noun*) hair that grows on a man's face in front of the ears.

sidewalk (*noun*) pavement beside street where people walk

slow down (*phrasal verb*) reduce the progress of

sneakers (*noun*) running shoes

species (*noun*) class of plants or animals that are related to each other

stairs (*noun*) steps leading from one floor to another in a building

stamp (*noun*) small square on an envelope that indicates the cost of delivering the item

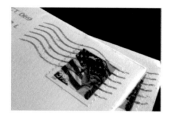

step on (*phrasal verb*) put feet on

store (*verb*) keep for later

suffer (*verb*) be sick

supply (*verb*) give, produce

swallow (*verb*) make food or drink pass down the throat

swollen (*adjective*) enlarged, expended

T

target (*noun used as adjective*) that you want to convince or inform

teen (*noun*) person between 13 and 19 years old

thoughts (*noun, plural*) ideas

throw away (*phrasal verb*) put in the garbage

toward (*preposition*) in the direction of

trap (*verb*) retain, prevent from escaping

treated (*adjective*) seen by a doctor

twisted (*adjective*) accidentally turned and injured

U

unhealthy (*adjective*) not healthy, bad for your health

unlike (*adjective*) not like, different

unsafe (*adjective*) not safe, dangerous

W

waistline (*noun*) middle of body

warranty (*noun*) guarantee

waste (*noun*) garbage

warming (*noun*) an increase in temperature

warm up (*verb*) increase in temperature

warning (*noun*) alert, recommendation about a possible danger

wet (*verb*) put water on

within (*preposition*) inside, not exceeding

word of mouth (*expression*) information passed on from one person to the next

MODULE C

A

according to (*adverb*) as recounted in

actually (*adverb*) in fact, really

afraid (*adjective*) scared

agreement (*noun*) entente

allowed (*adjective*) permitted

almost (*adverb*) nearly

although (*conjunction*) even if

around (*preposition*) near, close

ask out (*phrasal verb*) invite on a date

attractive (*adjective*) interesting

B

battle (*noun*) conflict

become (*verb*) start to be

beginning (*noun*) start

behind (*preposition*) in back of

believed (*adjective*) thought

belong to (*phrasal verb*) be owned by

between (*preposition*) in the middle of

blow out (*verb*) extinguish

boatswain (*noun*) officer responsible for operation of ship

booty (*noun*) stolen treasure

bring together (*phrasal verb*) unify, unite

bump (*verb*) knock

burn (*verb*) destroy by fire, copy to a CD or DVD

C

call on (*phrasal verb*) visit

carvings (*noun, plural*) designs cut into wood or stone

catchy (*adjective*) interesting and easy to remember

century (*noun*) period of 100 years

cheat (*verb*) do something dishonest

cheer (*verb*) shout and encourage

chores (*noun, plural*) tasks

claim (*noun*) say

clothed (*adjective*) wearing clothes

command (*verb*) control

complain (*verb*) express dissatisfaction

conduct (*noun*) comportment

run for **cover** (*expression*) hide, find a safe place

Crane Dance (*compound noun*) traditional dance

crew (*noun*) sailors on a ship

custom (*noun*) tradition

D

dating (*noun*) meeting regularly romantically

deck (*noun*) floor of boat

deserve (*verb*) merit

despite (*preposition*) even if

dice (*noun, plural*) small cubes with 1–6 dots on sides

dream of (*phrasal verb*) think about while sleeping

drinking water (*compound noun*) potable water

drop (*verb*) let fall, descend

E

elect (*verb*) select by voting

enough (*adjective*) sufficient

escape (*verb*) evade

F

fame (*noun*) celebrity

fate (*noun*) destiny

feared (*adjective*) making people afraid

fearful (*adjective*) frightening

feelings (*noun, plural*) emotions

fierce (*adjective*) ferocious

follow (*verb*) obey instructions

foremast (*noun*) pole where sails are attached

further (*adverb*) more

G

get used to (*phrasal verb*) become accustomed to, adapt to

greatly (*adverb*) very much

golden age (*noun*) period of time when something is popular

good grief (*expression*) Oh, no!

guest (*noun*) person invited

gunpowder (*noun*) explosive mixture

H

hand in (*phrasal verb*) give in

happen (*verb*) occur

harbour (*noun*) calm, safe waters near land

hard facts (*noun*) real truth

harmless (*adjective*) not dangerous, safe

heartless (*adjective*) without feeling or pity

helm (*noun*) wheel for guiding a boat

hide (*verb*) go where nobody can see you

hit it off (*phrasal verb*) enjoy being with

hold (*verb*) keep in hand

hope (*verb*) want, wish

hurt (*verb*) do damage

hurt (*adjective*) suffering from loss or damage

I

increasingly (*adverb*) more and more often

in front of (*prepositional phrase*) before

injure (*verb*) cause physical damage

injuries (*noun, plural*) damages to the body

island (*noun*) isle, land surrounded by water

K

keep an eye on (*phrasal verb*) watch over

keep a record (*phrasal verb*) write notes

keep on doing something (*phrasal verb*) do something repeatedly

keep watch (*phrasal verb*) do surveillance

kiss (*verb*) touch with lips

know-it-all (*compound noun*) person who thinks he/she knows everything

L

last (*verb*) endure, continue

last night (*expression*) the night before, yesterday night

at **least** (*adverbial phrase*) at the minimum

lend (*verb*) give temporarily

likeable (*adjective*) easy to like

likely (*adjective*) probable

make a **living** (*expression*) work

loaf (*noun*) a quantity of bread

locker (*noun*) compartment with a lock

lodge (*noun*) building, house

loonie (*noun*) one dollar coin

lovers (*noun*) people who are in love with each other

lucky in love (*expression*) successful in relationships

M

main (*adjective*) principal

matchmaking (*noun*) finding people to form couples

mate (*noun*) partner in a couple

meeting (*noun*) encounter

merchant (*adjective*) carrying merchandise

Middle Ages (*noun, plural*) period between the 5th century and the 14th century

N

Native American (*adjective*) Aboriginal

New World (*compound noun*) the Americas

notorious (*adjective*) famous for something bad

P

pay the price (*expression*) be penalized

pick up (*phrasal verb*) lift up, go get

pillow (*noun*) long cushion for resting head upon

plentiful (*adjective*) abundant

plunder (*verb*) steal goods or treasure

portray (*verb*) represent, impersonate

powerful (*adjective*) strong, efficient

pregnant (*adjective*) with child

in the **process** (*expression*) in the act

proposal (*noun*) offer

provide (*verb*) supply, furnish

Q

quartermaster (*noun*) ship's officer who furnishes equipment and pay

R

raid (*verb*) attack

rainstorm (*noun*) tempest with much rain

rather than (*adverb*) in preference to

reindeer (*noun*) large deer living in Arctic regions similar to caribou

release (*verb*) set free, liberate

rely on (*verb*) depend on

remain (*verb*) stay

restless (*adjective*) impatient

rules (*noun, plural*) regulations

run (*verb*) manage

S

sail (*noun*) piece of material to catch the wind

sail (*verb*) travel by boat

sailor (*noun*) mariner, worker on a ship

sales (*noun, plural*) quantity sold

Scotland (*noun*) country in United Kingdom to the north of England

in **search** of (*prepositional phrase*) looking for

secluded (*adjective*) isolated

setting (*noun*) area around

settler (*noun*) immigrant

set up (*phrasal verb*) organize

ship (*noun*) large boat

shoplift (*verb*) steal from a shop

the **sight** of (*noun*) view of

smoke (*noun*) carbon fumes from fire

sneak preview (*compound noun*) show before official opening

spend (*verb*) pass

sock hop (*compound noun*) dance

spread (*verb*) disseminate

steal (*verb*) rob, take

still (*adverb*) at a certain time

strange (*adjective*) bizarre

strength (*noun*) force, power

studies (*noun, plural*) research reports

submit (*verb*) obey, consent

suitable (*adjective*) appropriate

surrender (*verb*) cede

sweethearts (*noun, plural*) two people in love with each other

sword (*noun*) fighting armament with long blade

T

take care of (*phrasal verb*) look after

target (*noun*) object of attention

thirsty (*adjective*) in need of a drink

throughout (*preposition*) during the entire time

toss around (*phrasal verb*) move from side to side, up and down

trust (*verb*) be confident about

U

unbelievably (*adverb*) incredibly

upcoming (*adjective*) happening soon

upper (*adjective*) higher

V

vessel (*noun*) ship

W

wake up (*phrasal verb*) rouse from sleep

Wales (*noun*) country in the United Kingdom to the west of England

warn (*verb*) alert, draw attention

weapon (*noun*) armament

wedding day (*compound noun*) day of marriage

wife (*noun*) female spouse

without (*preposition*) not having

wonderful (*adjective*) marvellous

wrapped (*adjective*) enveloped

A

ability (*noun*) capability

addict (*noun*) person who needs or is enthusiastic about something

allowance (*noun*) allocation

allow (*verb*) permit

argue (*verb*) dispute, disagree

armpit (*noun*) underarm

attend (*verb*) be present at an event

aware (*adjective*) conscious

awesome (*adjective*) incredible

B

balance (*noun*) equilibrium

balance (*verb*) hold in equilibrium

battlefield (*noun*) place where military forces fight

beat (*verb*) hit

bother (*verb*) disturb, worry

boundary (*noun*) limit

building (*noun*) structure made by people to live or work in

build (*verb*) construct

bull (*noun*) male cow

bull runner (*noun*) person who runs away from the bulls

C

challenge (*noun*) something that is difficult and exciting

chat (*verb*) talk, have conversation

cheer (*verb*) shout encouragement

cheerfully (*adverb*) happily

chess (*noun*) a game of strategy

close behind (*expression*) to the rear and not far away

complain (*verb*) express dissatisfaction, protest

crowd (*noun*) large group of people, spectators

D

dedicated (*adjective*) committed

defy (*verb*) challenge

deserve (*verb*) merit

disastrous (*adjective*) extremely dangerous, maybe fatal, catastrophic

disgusting (*adjective*) very unpleasant

downtown (*noun*) city centre

drums (*noun*) percussion instruments

E

earn a living (*expression*) work for money (to live on)

elderly (*noun*) older people

effective (*adjective*) producing the desired result

enough (*adjective*) sufficient

ensure (*verb*) guarantee

errand (*noun*) a short voyage to get something

event (*noun*) occasion, happening

excitement (*noun*) strong happy or nervous feeling

exhausting (*adjective*) very tiring

F

fall (*noun*) autumn

fast (*adjective*) quick

fear (*noun*) anxiety, feeling of being afraid

fight (*verb*) combat

finish line (*compound noun*) line that competitors need to traverse to win

first aid (*compound noun*) medical assistance before seeing a doctor

floor (*noun*) level

focused (*adjective*) concentrated

freedom (*noun*) liberty

free fall (*compound noun*) descent without an open parachute

frightening (*adjective*) scary, causing fear

G

German (*adjective*) person from Germany

get ready (*phrasal verb*) prepare yourself

goal (*noun*) objective

grades (*noun*) school results

grow (*verb*) get bigger

H

handle (*verb*) manage, deal with

happen (*verb*) occur

head (*verb*) go in the direction of

heart (*noun*) organ in body that pumps blood

heavy in the air (*expression*) strongly present, noticeable

height (*noun*) distance above the ground, tallness

highly (*adverb*) very

hike (*noun*) walk, climb

hill (*noun*) a high area, smaller than a mountain

however (*adverb*) in spite of this

huge (*adjective*) very big

hurt (*adjective*) injured, damaged

I

ice (*noun*) frozen water

involved (*adjective*) implicated

ironworker (*noun*) person who works with iron or steel

J

jump (*noun*) leap, bound into the air, leave the ground

K

keep (*verb*) maintain, ensure that something remains or stays

L

land (*noun*) surface of the earth, soil

laws (*noun*) regulations

lifeguard (*noun*) expert swimmer who watches and helps other swimmers

look closely (*phrasal verb*) examine carefully

luck (*noun*) fortune, success

M

make your way (*expression*) proceed, go forward

meant to (*adjective*) supposed to

meet (*verb*) encounter

mentally challenged (*expression*) having problems with some mental functions

mountain bike (*noun*) strong bicycle for riding off-road

mow the lawn (*expression*) cut the grass

N

near (*verb*) approach

nickname (*noun*) alternate name

noise (*noun*) loud sound

no matter what (*expression*) in spite of everything

notice (*verb*) remark

O

outdoors (*adverb*) outside (of buildings)

out there (*expression*) anywhere, everywhere

over (*preposition*) more than

overseas (*adjective*) across the ocean, on another continent

own (*adjective*) belonging to you

P

pick up (*phrasal verb*) collect

poor (*noun*) those having very little money or goods

posted (*adjective*) placed, put onto

pretty (*adverb*) very

previous (*adjective*) the one before

push yourself to the limit (*expression*) go as far as you can

R

race (*noun*) speed contest

rattlesnake (*noun*) poisonous serpent

reach (*verb*) attain

really (*adverb*) truly

reef (*noun*) a body of rock or coral at or near the surface of the ocean

reliable (*adjective*) dependable

remember (*verb*) recall / not forget

remote (*adjective*) distant

requested (*adjective*) asked for

retrieve (*verb*) recuperate

ride down (*verb*) descend

rush (*noun*) intense feeling of excitement

S

safety (*noun*) security

scene (*noun*) area where something is

Scotland (*noun*) country in the UK to the north of England

Scottish (*adjective*) coming from Scotland

scuba (*adjective*) concerning or using equipment for breathing underwater

senior (*noun*) older person

sensible (*adjective*) using wisdom and logic, reasonable

set a record (*expression*) establish a new record

share (*verb*) have in common

shelter (*noun*) haven, refuge

ship (*verb*) send

shout (*verb*) call out, cry out

shove (*verb*) push suddenly and roughly

show (*verb*) display, present / prove to

show off (*phrasal verb*) display proudly

be sick (*verb*) vomit

sightseeing (*noun*) visiting the interesting places in a town, city, etc.

skill (*noun*) talent

sky walker (*compound noun*) person who does construction work on very tall buildings

slip (*verb*) fall, slide

slippery (*adjective*) smooth and easy to slide on

smooth (*adjective*) with no bumps, not abrasive or rough

snorkelling (*noun*) using a tube for breathing in the water

Spaniard (*noun*) person from Spain

speed (*noun*) rapidity, velocity

speed (*verb*) move rapidly

stand for (*verb*) represent, mean

state (*verb*) indicate, mention

still (*adverb*) in spite of this

stuck (*adjective*) unable to move or get free

stunt (*noun*) dangerous act

suddenly (*adverb*) quickly and without warning

suffer (*verb*) be affected negatively

support (*verb*) encourage

T

take part in (*phrasal verb*) participate in

tasty (*adjective*) having a good taste or flavour

thrill (*noun*) excitement

throughout (*preposition*) across, all over

tough (*adjective*) hard, difficult

toward (*adverb*) in the direction of

turn up for (*phrasal verb*) come to see or participate in

tutor (*noun*) private teacher

U

unbelieveable (*adjective*) incredible, difficult to imagine

upon us (*expression*) here

used (*adjective*) employed

usually (*adverb*) normally

V

vile (*adjective*) really horrible

volunteer (*adjective*) unpaid

volunteer (*noun*) person who works for no pay

W

watch your step (*expression*) be careful where you walk

weigh (*verb*) have a certain heaviness

whether (*adverb*) if

winner (*verb*) victor

wish (*verb*) want

without (*preposition*) not having

world (*adjective*) referring to the entire planet Earth and all of humanity

ANTHOLOGY

A

across (*preposition*) against

ahead (*adverb*) before

apologize (*verb*) say sorry

B

bake sale (*compound noun*) sale of baked goods to raise money for charity

become of (*verb*) happen to

besides (*preposition*) apart from, in addition to

beware (*verb*) be careful

boil over (*phrasal verb*) what happens when heated water spills out of its container

bore into (*verb*) penetrate

broaden (*verb*) make wider

bully (*noun*) person who intimidates a weaker person

burn a hole in your pocket (*expression*) make it impossible for you to ignore something

C

call it off (*phrasal verb*) terminate a relationship

cheek (*noun*) jowl, side of face below the eye

clutch (*verb*) take a tight hold

cozy (*adjective*) comfortable

cure (*verb*) make better

D

dare (*verb*) have the courage

dazed (*adjective*) confused

deaf (*adjective*) not being able to hear

deed (*noun*) action

dig into (*phrasal verb*) put hand into

disease (*noun*) malady

dismay (*noun*) despair, discouragement

drift (*verb*) float

drip (*verb*) be very wet, with liquid on the surface

drop (*verb*) descend, fall or lose hold, let fall

drown (*verb*) die by breathing in water

E

enrol (*verb*) register

F

farther (*adverb*) more

few (*adjective*) of limited number

forehead (*noun*) part of face above the eyes

forever (*adverb*) for all time

forgetful (*adjective*) doesn't always remember things

freak (*noun*) something orsomeone very different from the norm

freeze (*verb*) stay immobile

fringe (*adjective*) belonging to those from the unpopular group

frown (*noun*) expression of disapproval

G

gather (*verb*) collect

gifted (*adjective*) those with talent

glance (*verb*) look quickly

go by (*phrasal verb*) pass

go for (*phrasal verb*) like

grab (*verb*) take quickly

groan (*verb*) make a sound of displeasure

H

hardly (*adverb*) barely

harmless (*adjective*) not dangerous, doesn't hurt

head (*verb*) go in the direction of

heal (*verb*) cure, make better

hearing ear dog (*compound noun*) dog trained to help deaf people

I

in-crowder (*noun*) part of the popular group

interfere with (*verb*) obstruct, upset

L

lap (*verb*) noise of water moving

leak (*verb*) pass through a hole

lean back (*verb*) lie back

leap (*verb*) jump

lie (*verb*) say something that is not true

M

make it through (*phrasal verb*) endure

make up your mind (*expression*) decide

meanness (*noun*) unkindness, cruelty

mean well (*expression*) have good intentions

N

nod (*verb*) say yes by moving the head

O

once (*adverb*) one time

otherwise (*adverb*) something else

P

peer (*verb*) look hard

plain as day (*expression*) very clear

pull out (*verb*) drive out

R

raise money (*expression*) collect money for a charitable cause

reach (*verb*) get to

report card (*compound noun*) document to show school results

run (*verb*) manage

S

sharp (*adjective*) clear

shiver (*verb*) tremble because of the cold

shrug (*verb*) move shoulders up and down to show that you don't know

since (*conjunction*) because

stammer (*verb*) hesitate when speaking because of nerves

stare (*verb*) look

steadily (*adverb*) without changing speed

stream (*noun*) small river

struggle (*verb*) work hard at something difficult

surrender (*verb*) give in, yield

surroundings (*noun*) environment around you

T

tell (*verb*) say to / understand

trust (*verb*) have confidence in

U

used to (*verb*) did

W

weave (*verb*) move though a crowd of people

whether (*adverb*) if

whole (*adjective*) entire

wicked (*adjective*) mean

within (*preposition*) inside, not outside

no **wonder** (*expression*) it's no surprise

wonder (*verb*) ask yourself

wrap around (*phrasal verb*) surround

The Simple Present Tense

Use the simple present to describe:

- A routine
  I **jog** every day before school.

- A fact or description
  The movie **is** very funny.

- Possession
  They **have** many techniques to relieve stress.

- Likes and dislikes
  George **likes** to eat fruit every day.
  Francine **doesn't like** to exercise.

- These discourse markers are often used with the simple present tense:
  every day, always, often, frequently, sometimes, regularly, never, from time to time

Forming the simple present

To be

Affirmative

Subject	Verb	Rest of sentence
She	is	a positive person.
I **am** / I'm		very nervous.
You **are** / You're		calm.
He **is** / He's		stressed out.
She **is** / She's		sleepy.
It **is** / It's		a good way to relax.
We **are** / We're		worried about the exam.
They **are** / They're		healthy.

Negative

Subject	Verb + not	Rest of sentence
She	**is not**	a positive person.
I **am not** / I'm **not** very nervous.		
You **are not** / You're **not** / You **aren't** calm.		
He **is not** / He's **not** / He **isn't** stressed out.		
She **is not** / She's **not** / She **isn't** sleepy.		
It **is not** / It's **not** / It **isn't** a good way to relax.		
We **are not** / We're **not** / We **aren't** worried …		
They **are not** / They're **not** / They **aren't** …		

Other verbs

Affirmative

Subject	Verb	Rest of sentence
I	love	fruit.
You	eat	too much junk.
He/She/It	likes	music.
We	run	every day.
They	watch	fish swim by.

Negative

Subject	do/does + not + verb	Rest of sentence
I	**do not** / **don't love**	fruit.
You	**do not** / **don't eat**	too much junk.
He/She/It	**does not** / **doesn't like**	music.
We	**do not** / **don't run**	every day.
They	**do not** / **don't watch**	fish swim by.

SPELL WELL

- Notice the spelling for the third-person singular in the simple present:
  She read**s**.   He make**s**.   It rain**s**.
- Remember to add **es** to verbs that end in **ch, sh, o, s, x** or **z**.
  She rela<u>x</u>**es** regularly.
  He fini<u>sh</u>**es** his homework before playing sports.
  He wat<u>ch</u>**es** funny movies.
- Remember to change the **y** to **ies** when the verb ends in a **consonant + y**.
  She stu<u>d</u>**ies** every day.   He t<u>r</u>**ies** to stay positive.
- Notice the verb **to have**:
  I/You/We/They **have** …   BUT   He/She/It **has** …
- Notice the apostrophe in the contracted form. It replaces the missing letter or letters:
  I am → **I'm** (the apostrophe replaces the **a**)
  We are → **We're** (the apostrophe replaces the **a**)
  She is not → **She isn't** (the apostrophe replaces the **o**)

Asking questions in the simple present

To be

Yes/no questions

Verb	Subject	Rest of sentence
Am	I	ready for the exam?
Are	you	positive about the project?
Is	he/she	a funny person?
Are	we	happy about our choice?
Are	they	ready for the competition?

Information questions

QW*	Verb	Subject	Rest of sentence
How far	**am**	I	from the gym?
Why	**are**	you	here?
What	**is**	it?	
Where	**are**	we?	
How	**are**	they	now?

Other verbs

Yes/no questions

Do/Does	Subject	Verb	Rest of question
Do	I	**need**	to worry?
Do	you	**eat**	fruit every day?
Does	he/she	**exercise**	every week?
Do	we	**know**	the solution?
Do	they	**laugh**	often?

Information questions

QW*	do/does	Subject	Verb	Rest of question
Where	**do**	I	**eat**	my lunch?
What	**do**	you	**do**	to relax?
Why	**does**	he/she	**study**	every night?
How	**do**	we	**know**	what to do?
When	**do**	they	**leave**	for school?

* QW = question word.

The Present Continuous

Use the present continuous to describe:

- An action that is happening now. The action began before the present time and will continue some time after the present.
  The movie **is playing** now.
- Actions that take place over a period of time:
  She**'s relaxing** on the beach this summer.
- Actions that are sure to take place in the future.
  Jane **is playing** soccer tomorrow.
- These discourse markers are often used with the present continuous:
  right now, at the moment, today, this week, this month, this year, for the time being, presently, currently

Forming the present continuous

Affirmative

Subject	*Verb* to be + ing *verb*	*Rest of sentence*	*With contracted form of* to be
I	**am relaxing**	at the beach.	I**'m relaxing** …
You	**are watching**	too much TV.	You**'re watching** …
He/She	**is sleeping in**	this weekend.	He**'s**/She**'s sleeping in** …
It	**is raining**	outside right now.	It**'s raining** …
We	**are training**	for the competition.	We**'re training** for …
They	**are doing**	their homework.	They**'re doing** …

Negative

Subject	*Verb* to be + *not* + ing *verb*	*Rest of sentence*	*With contracted form of* to be
I	**am not relaxing**	at the beach.	I**'m not relaxing** …
You	**are not watching**	too much TV.	You**'re not watching** / You **aren't** …
He/She	**is not sleeping in**	this weekend.	He**'s**/She**'s not** … / He/She **isn't** …
It	**is not raining**	outside right now.	It**'s not raining** … / It **isn't** …
We	**are not training**	for the competition.	We**'re not training** … / We **aren't** …
They	**are not doing**	their homework.	They**'re not doing** … / They **aren't** …

SPELL WELL

Notice that, when forming the present continuous:
- verbs ending in **e** drop the **e** before adding -**ing**: giv<u>e</u> → giv**ing**, tak<u>e</u> → tak**ing**
- verbs ending in a consonant double the final consonant: si<u>t</u> → sit**ting**, ru<u>n</u> → run**ning**
- verbs ending in **ie** change the **ie** to **y** before -**ing**: l<u>ie</u> → **lying**, d<u>ie</u> → d**ying**

Asking questions in the present continuous

Yes/no questions

Verb to be	*Subject*	*-ing verb*	*Rest of question*	**Short answers** *(Contracted form)*
Am	I	**studying**	with you?	Yes, you **are**. / No, you **are not** (**aren't**).
Are	you	**watching**	a funny movie?	Yes, I am. / No, I **am not** (**I'm not**).
Is	he	**bringing**	his dog with him?	Yes he is. / No, he **is not** (**isn't**).
Is	it	**barking**	at the birds?	Yes, it is. / No, it **is not** (**isn't**).
Are	we	**eating**	fruit salad for dessert?	Yes. we are. / No, we **are not** (**aren't**).
Are	they	**walking**	in the forest now?	Yes, they are. / No, they **are not** (**aren't**).

Information questions

*QW**	*Verb* to be	*Subject*	*-ing verb*	*Rest of question*
When	**am**	I	**playing**	my next game?
Why	**are**	you	**sleeping**	in class?
How	**is**	he/she	**going**	to the soccer practice?
Where	**are**	we	**eating?**	
What	**are**	they	**watching**	on TV?

* QW = question word.

The Simple Past Tense

Use the simple past to describe a situation or an action that happened in the past and was completed in the past.

Yesterday, I **wrote** a biology exam.

Last night I **watched** a documentary about the brain.

- These discourse markers are often used with the simple past:
  yesterday, last week, last night, last month, last year, two weeks ago

Forming the simple past

With the verb *to be*

Affirmative

Subject	*Verb*	*Rest of sentence*
I	**was**	at the soccer game.
You	**were**	happy with the result.
He/She	**was**	absent yesterday.
It	**was**	cloudy this morning.
We	**were**	at the practice.
They	**were**	tired after the game.

Negative

Subject	*Verb + not*	*Rest of sentence*
I	**was not / wasn't**	at the soccer game.
You	**were not/weren't**	happy with the result.
He/She	**was not / wasn't**	absent yesterday.
It	**was not / wasn't**	cloudy this morning.
We	**were not / weren't**	at the practice.
They	**were not / weren't**	tired after the game.

Forming the simple past, cont'd

With other verbs

Affirmative of regular verbs

Subject	Verb	Rest of sentence
I	**liked**	skating.
You	**needed**	more sleep.
He	**jogged**	yesterday.
She	**talked**	to her parents.
We	**asked**	for help.
They	**cooked**	healthy meals.

Affirmative of irregular verbs
- Irregular verbs do not end in **ed**. Their form changes and must be learned:*
  go = went   leave = left   fly = flew

Negative of regular verbs

Subject	did not/didn't + verb	Rest of sentence
I	**did not / didn't like**	skating.
You	**did not / didn't need**	more sleep.
He	**did not / didn't jog**	yesterday.
She	**did not / didn't talk**	to her parents.
We	**did not / didn't ask**	for help.
They	**did not / didn't cook**	healthy meals.

Negative of regular verbs

I	**did not / didn't go**	to soccer practice.
She	**did not / didn't leave**	until 10:30 that night.
They	**did not / didn't fly**	to Vancouver.

* See p. 190 for a list of irregular verbs

SPELL WELL

- Form the simple past of **regular verbs** by adding **ed** to the verb:
  walk = walk**ed**   cook = cook**ed**

- If the verb ends in **e**, just add **d**:
  love = lov**ed**   skate = skat**ed**

- For verbs that end in a consonant + **y**, change the **y** to **ied**:
  stud**y** = stud**ied**   try = tr**ied**

SAY IT WELL

When you use the simple past, the **–ed** ending can have three different sounds:

D as in rained (rain-**d**)
T as in stopped (stop-**t**)
ID as in divided (divide-**id**)

Asking questions in the simple past

To be

Yes/no questions

Verb	Subject	Rest of question
Was	I	ready for the exam?
Were	you	positive about the project?
Was	he	a funny person?
Was	she	nervous about the test?
Were	we	happy about our choice?
Were	they	ready for the competition?

Information questions

QW*	Verb	Subject	Rest of question
Where	**was**	I	yesterday?
When	**were**	you	in Toronto?
What	**was**	she	like when then?
Why	**was**	he	so excited?
Who	**were**	we	supposed to meet?
How long	**were**	they	at the show?

Other verbs

Yes/no questions

Did	Subject	Verb	Rest of question
Did	I	**buy**	the book?
Did	you	**see**	the new movie?
Did	he	**go**	to the restaurant?
Did	it	**take**	a long time?
Did	we	**meet**	them last year?
Did	they	**find**	the address?

Information questions

QW*	did	Subject	Verb	Rest of question
Where	**did**	I	**put**	the project?
What	**did**	you	**speak**	about with Paul?
Why	**did**	she	**take**	the puppy?
How	**did**	it	**run**	away?
When	**did**	we	**sell**	the house?
Who	**did**	they	**choose**	for their team?

* QW = question word.

Common Irregular Verbs

Base form	Simple past
babysit	babysat
be (am/is/are)	was/were
beat	beat
become	became
begin	began
bend	bent
bet	bet
bite	bit
bleed	bled
blow	blew
break	broke
bring	brought
build	built
burst	burst
buy	bought
catch	caught
choose	chose
come	came
cost	cost
creep	crept
cut	cut
deal	dealt
dig	dug
dive	dived/dove
do	did
draw	drew
drink	drank
drive	drove
eat	ate
fall	fell
feed	fed
feel	felt
fight	fought
find	found

Base form	Simple past
forget	forgot
forgive	forgave
freeze	froze
get	got
give	gave
go	went
grow	grew
hang	hung
have	had
hear	heard
hide	hid
hit	hit
hold	held
hurt	hurt
keep	kept
kneel	knelt
know	knew
lay	laid
lead	led
leave	left
lend	lent
let	let
lie (down)	lay
lose	lost
make	made
mean	meant
meet	met
pay	paid
put	put
read	read
ride	rode
ring	rang
run	ran
say	said

Base form	Simple past
see	saw
sell	sold
send	sent
shine	shined/shone
shoot	shot
shrink	shank
shut	shut
sing	sang
sink	sank
sit	sat
sleep	slept
slide	slid
speak	spoke
spend	spent
split	split
stand	stood
steal	stole
sting	stung
stink	stank
strike	struck
sweep	swept
swim	swam
take	took
teach	taught
tear	tore
tell	told
think	thought
throw	threw
understand	understood
wake	woke
wear	wore
win	won
write	wrote

The Past Continuous

Use the past continuous:

- To describe an action that was in progress at a specific moment in the past:
  We **were researching** our project when we lost power.
  She **was looking** for her glasses when I met her.
  Notice how the past continuous is often used in conjunction with the simple past.

- To show that two actions were happening simultaneously in the past:
  While we **were downloading** the music, the boys **were preparing** the visuals.

Forming the past continuous

Affirmative

Subject	Past of verb to be + -ing verb	Rest of sentence
I	**was trying on**	some platform shoes.
You	**were talking**	about the hoola-hoop craze.
He/She	**was listening**	to a radio show.
It	**was getting**	difficult to follow the trends.
We/They	**were hanging out**	at the arcade.

Negative

Subject	Past of verb to be + not + -ing verb	Rest of sentence
I	**was not enjoying**	my in-line skating lesson.
You	**were not looking**	at the hybrid car.
He/She	**was not taking**	good notes for the project.
It	**was not working out**	very well.
We/They	**were not recycling**	enough.

SPELL WELL

Notice that, when forming the past continuous:

- verbs ending in **e** drop the **e** before adding **ing**:
  mak<u>e</u> → mak**ing**,
  leav<u>e</u> → leav**ing**

- verbs ending in a consonant double the final consonant:
  swi<u>m</u> → swim**ming**,
  cu<u>t</u> → cut**ting**

- verbs ending in **ie** change the **ie** to **y** before **ing**:
  l<u>ie</u> → **lying**, t<u>ie</u> → t**ying**

Asking questions in the past continuous

Yes/no questions

Past of to be	Subject	-ing verb	Rest of question
Was	I	**going out**	with Max then?
Were	you	**working**	on the design for a long time?
Was	he/she/it	**making**	progress?
Were	we/they	**dating**	at that point?

Information questions

QW*	Past of to be	Subject	-ing verb	Rest of question
What	**was**	I	**doing**	on Tuesday morning?
Who	**was**	she	**meeting**	last night?
Why	**were**	you	**looking**	for a recycling centre?
Where	**were**	they	**coming**	from?

* QW = question word.

The Future

Use the **future simple** to talk about a probable future action or situation.
Use the **future with** *going to* to talk about an intention or to make a prediction.

Forming the future simple

Affirmative

Subject	will	Verb	Rest of sentence	Contracted forms
I	will	**write up**	my CV at some point.	**I'll write** up …
You	will	**enjoy**	the movie.	**You'll enjoy** …
He/She/It	will	**travel**	to the moon someday.	**He'll/She'll/It'll travel** …
We/They	will	**plan**	their trip carefully.	**We'll/They'll plan** …

Negative

Subject	will + not	Verb	Rest of sentence	Contracted forms
I	**will not**	**take**	the bus with you.	I **won't take** …
You	**will not**	**have**	time for a shower.	You **won't have** …
He/She/It	**will not**	**find**	the toy in the box.	He/She/It **won't find** …
We/They	**will not**	**present**	their project today.	We/They **won't present** …

Asking questions in the future simple

Yes/no questions

Will	Subject	Verb	Rest of Sentence
Will	*Subject*	*Verb*	*Rest of Sentence*
Will	I	**get**	a place at college?
Will	you	**go**	to university?
Will	he/she/it	**pass**	the stress test?
Will	we/they	**come**	to a consensus?

Information questions

QW*	will	Subject	Verb	Rest of question
*QW**	*will*	*Subject*	*Verb*	*Rest of question*
Where	**will**	I	**go**	to college?
How	**will**	you	**get**	there?
When	**will**	he	**take**	the driving test?
What	**will**	we	**need**	for the trip?

(see bottom of page)

Forming the future with *going to*

Affirmative

Subject	Verb to be + going to + verb	Rest of sentence	Contracted forms
Subject	*Verb* to be + *going to* + *verb*	*Rest of sentence*	*Contracted forms*
I	**am going to help**	my father on Sunday.	I**'m going to** …
You	**are going to buy**	a hybrid car.	You**'re going to** …
He/She/It	**is going to work**	out later.	He**'s**/She**'s**/It**'s going to** …
We/They	**are going to travel**	this summer.	We**'re**/They**'re going to** …

Negative

Subject	Verb to be + not + going to + verb	Rest of sentence	Contracted forms
Subject	*Verb* to be + *not* + *going to* + *verb*	*Rest of sentence*	*Contracted forms*
I	**am not going to take**	the train.	I**'m not** …
You	**are not going to share**	the driving.	You**'re not** / You **aren't** …
He/She/It	**is not going to come**	today.	He**'s not** / He **isn't** …
We/They	**are not going to get**	married this year.	We**'re not** / We **aren't** …

Asking questions in the future with *going to*

Yes/no questions

Verb to be	Subject	going to + verb	Rest of question
Verb to be	*Subject*	*going to* + *verb*	*Rest of question*
Am	I	**going to have**	time?
Are	you	**going to revise**	the document?

Information questions

QW*	Verb to be	Subject	going to + verb	Rest of question
*QW**	*Verb* to be	*Subject*	*going to* + *verb*	*Rest of question*
What	**is**	he	**going to do**	after high school?
Where	**are**	they	**going to live**	next year?

* QW = question word.

Words ending in -ING

Use **words ending in -ing** as adjectives, nouns or verbs:
- **Adjective**
  Music can have a **calming** effect. (The adjective **calming** describes the type of effect.)
- **Noun**
  Walking is a benefit to your health. (The noun **walking** is the subject of the sentence.)
- **Verb**
  Stef **is watching** a movie. (The continuous tenses use the verb *to be* + verb in **–ing**.)

Questions in the Present, Past and Future

Question words

Use question words to ask for information about:

people	Who
things	What
location	Where
time, date	When
reason	Why
choice of people/thing	Which

manner	How
quantity (non count)	How much
quantity (count)	How many
length, time	How long
frequency	How often
age	How old

Questions in the simple present

	QW*	do/does	Subject	Verb	Rest of question
Information questions	Who**	do	I	resemble?	
	Where	does	she	work	these days?
Yes/no questions		Does	it	take	a long time to repair?
		Do	we	need	help?

** See note below.

Questions in the simple past

	QW*	did**	Subject	Verb	Rest of question
Information questions	What	did	I	borrow	from you?
	How much	did	she	pay	for her new bike?
Yes/no questions		Did	it	snow	last night?
		Did	they	ask	for assistance?

* QW = question word.
** Do not use *do* or *did* when *who* or *what* are the **subject** of the sentence.
    Who **did** you **walk** to the park with?   Who **walks** the dog in your family?
    What **did** your sister **make** for supper?   What **made** that funny noise?

Questions in the future simple

	QW*	will	Subject	Verb	Rest of question
Information questions	When	will	I	see	you again?
	Why	will	they	miss	the party?
Yes/no questions		Will	she	take	the bus?
		Will	we	rent	the new pirate movie?

Questions with the verb *to be*

Simple present				
	QW*	Verb to be	Subject	Rest of question
Information questions	Where	are	you?	
	Why	is	he	unhappy?
Yes/no questions		Is	she	enthusiastic?
		Are	we	in the same group?

Simple past				
	QW*	Verb to be	Subject	Rest of question
Information questions	Why	was	I	so tired?
	How	was	she	when you saw her?
Yes/no questions		Were	they	in pain?
		Was	it	worth the effort?

Future simple					
	QW*	Verb to be	Subject	be	Rest of question
Information questions	How old	will	I	be	in 2035?
	Where	will	they	be	in 30 years?
Yes/no questions		Will	you	be	the same?
		Will	we	be	different?

* QW = question word.

Modals

Use modal auxiliaries to express ability, possibility or obligation. They can also be used to make suggestions and give advice.

Affirmative

Ability
- Can — Discussing things with a partner **can** help you think of new ideas.
- Be able to — These days, young people **are able to** date.

Possibility
- Might — My parents might buy a more energy-efficient car.
- May — We may not see the full effects of global warming for a while.

Obligation
- Must — She must study for her test.
- Have to — She has to take driving lessons to get her license.

Suggestion
- Should — You should get a good night of sleep before your exam tomorrow.
- Could — You could also listen to some relaxing music beforehand.

Negative

- To form the negative, simply add **not** between the modal and the verb:

  I **must not worry** so much. (I **mustn't worry** …)
  You **cannot watch** TV late at night. (You **can't watch** …)
  He **might not know** the best way to study.
  It **may not be** the best way to study.

- Note the contacted versions of **must not** and **cannot**: **mustn't** and **can't**.

Asking questions with modals

QW*	Modal	Subject	verb	Rest of question
When	**can**	I	**see**	the teacher for help?
Where	**should**	we	**have**	lunch?
	Could	you	**explain**	this assignment to me?
	May	we	**finish**	this project next week?

- The modals *have to* and *be able to* are exceptions. They follow the pattern used for *to have* and *to be*.
  Do they **have to stay** up so late at night?
  Are they **able to remember** all those historical dates?

* QW = question word.

SPELL WELL

Notice the apostrophe in the contracted form of some modals. It replaces the missing letter or letters:
must not → **mustn't** (the apostrophe replaces the **o**)
should not → **shouldn't** (the apostrophe replaces the **o**)
cannot → **can't** (the apostrophe replaces the **no**)

Conditionals: Expressing Real Conditions

Use a conditional structure to talk about what can or will happen in certain situations.

- Real conditions refer to events or situations that are possible, probable or certain.
- A conditional sentence has two parts: the if-clause, which presents the condition, and the main clause, which indicates the result.

Condition	Result
If I eat too much,	I will get sick. (probability)
If I eat too much,	I get sick. (certainty)

Notice that the if-clause must be in the present tense to express a real condition. The verb in the main (result) clause changes depending on the meaning you want to express.

Affirmative statements

- Look at the different meanings expressed by changing the verb in the main (result) clause:

  Condition: If we **download** music from the net,

  Results: we **are** in the wrong. (simple present = certainty)
  we **will be** in trouble. (future simple = probability)
  we **might ruin** an artist's career. (modal *might* = possibility)
  we **could regret** it later. (modal *could* = possibility)
  we **should** still **pay** for it. (modal *should* = suggestion)

- Notice that the if-clause can be placed before or after the main clause. When it is before, we separate the two clauses with a comma.

  If people recycle on a more regular basis, the planet will have a chance to recover.
                      Condition   Result
  The planet will have a chance to recover if people recycle on a more regular basis.
                      Result   Condition

Negative Statements

- Both the if-clause and the main (result) clause can contain a negative statement.
  If we do not look after the Earth's resources, our children will not have a planet to call home.

Questions

- If-clauses can also be used to ask questions about real conditions.
  Where will our children live if we destroy the Earth?

Adjectives and Adverbs

Use **adjectives** to describe a noun or pronoun.

- Adjectives are placed before a noun.
  The popularity of **extreme** sports is growing.
               adj.   noun
- Adjectives are also placed after the verbs *to be, to become* and *to seem*. These verbs link the adjective to the noun or pronoun they describe:
  These sports are **fun** to watch but they are very **dangerous**.
      noun   adj.   pronoun adj.
- In English, an adjective has no gender and is never plural.
  An **energetic** girl, an **energetic** boy, **energetic** students

- Some adjectives are more commonly used for females, others for males:
  a **beautiful** girl, a **handsome** man

- Nouns can also be used as adjectives. They are placed before the noun that they modify and are usually singular.
  Water polo is a difficult sport. **Fly** fishing is relaxing.

Use **adverbs** to modify a verb, adjective, another adverb or a complete sentence.

- An adverb can modify an adjective. The adverb is placed before the adjective.
  Sara finds her summer job **really** interesting.
                            adv.   adj.
- An adverb can modify a verb. Its position varies, depending on the type of adverb.

- Adverbs of time are usually placed at the beginning or end of the sentence.
  She has a new summer job **now**.
                       adv
- Adverbs of frequency are usually placed before the verb with simple present and past tenses.
  She **usually** works five hours a day.
     adv.   verb
- Adverbs of manner can be placed after the verb or before it.
  Sarah does her job **well**. She **carefully** follows instructions.
     verb   adv.   adv.   verb
- An adverb can modify another adverb. The modifying adverb is placed before the adverb it modifies.
  She works **very** quickly.
          adv. adv.
- An adverb can modify a complete sentence. The adverb is usually placed at the beginning of the sentence.
  Unfortunately, the job does not pay much.
     adv.

Types of adverbs

There are adverbs of degree, frequency, manner, place or position, and time.

Degree → He is **very** loud.

Frequency → I **often** read books.

Manner → She writes **carefully**.

Place or position → She is **upstairs**.

Time → They'll arrive **late**.

Forming adverbs of manner

• Adverbs of manner answer the question "How?".

• Many adjectives can become adverbs of manner by adding **-ly**.

Peter is a **careful** skateboarder. → He skateboards **carefully**.

            adj.   adv.

• There are some exceptions:

Adjective		Adverb	
good	→	well	Mila is a **good** climber. She climbs **well**.
hard	→	hard	George is a **hard** worker. He works **hard**.
fast	→	fast	Ian is a **fast** skater. He skates **fast**.

The Superlative Form

Use the superlative form of **adjectives** or **adverbs** to compare three or more things.

Adjectives

• To form the superlative, use **the** + adjective + **est** for adjectives of one syllable and most adjectives of two syllables.

The **coolest** job   the **happiest** employees

• For adjectives of three or more syllables and adjectives of two syllables ending in ful or re, use the most + adjective

The **most dangerous** job   the **most wonderful** summer job

SPELL WELL

• For adjectives that end in **y**, change it to **i** before adding **–est**

funny → the funniest   friendly → the friendliest

• For one-syllable adjectives ending in a vowel plus consonant, double the consonant before adding **–est**

big → the biggest   fat → the fattest

Adverbs

- To form the superlative of adverbs ending in **–ly**, use **the + most**.
  carefully → the most carefully   rapidly → the most rapidly

- For adverbs with the same form as the adjective, use **the** + adverb + **–est**
  hard → the hardest   soon → the soonest

- For some irregular adverbs, forms simply need to be learned.
  well → the best   far → the farthest

The Imperative

Use the imperative to:
- Give advice or make suggestions   Don't stress about the exam.
- Make requests (use *please* with the imperative)   Please turn off the TV.
- Give orders and commands   Stand up.
- Give warnings   Be careful!
- Give directions and instructions   Turn left at the first stop sign.

Forming the imperative

Affirmative

Base form of verb   *Rest of sentence*
Wash   your hands.
Eat   your vegetables.

Negative

Do not + base form of verb   *Rest of sentence*
Do not forget   your homework.
Don't watch   TV all night.

Notice that no subject is used with the imperative.

Active Voice or Passive Voice

- **In an active structure** the subject does the action.
  JK Rowling wrote the Harry Potter books.
     subject   verb   object

- **In a passive structure** the subject does not do the action. The subject receives the action.
  The Harry Potter books were written by JK Rowling.
     subject   verb   object

- Form verbs in the passive voice by using the appropriate tense and person of the verb **to be** + the **past participle of the verb**.

Active	**Passive**
John **welcomes** the guests.	The guests **are welcomed** by John.
We **use** a thermometer to take temperature.	A thermometer **is used** to take temperature.
Native Americans **built** skyscrapers.	Many skyscrapers **were built** by Native Americans.
They **cancelled** the picnic.	The picnic **was cancelled**.

Possessive Adjectives and Pronouns

Possessive adjectives and pronouns show possession. Possessive adjectives go before a noun and show who the noun belongs to. Possessive pronouns also show ownership but stand alone

Adjectives

This is **my** bag.
Your files are on the table.
Matt forgot **his** sweater.
Jessy loves **her** dog.
The dog wagged **its** tail.
Our house is amazing.
Their door is blue.

Pronouns

The bag is **mine**
Are these **yours**?
This is not my case, it's **his**.
Joanna doesn't like **hers** too much.

Ours is an amazing house.
The house with the blue door is **theirs**.

Remember that the possessive adjective or pronoun agrees with the person and not the object.
The green bag belongs to Alex. I like **his** bag.
The blue bag belongs to Jenny. I like **hers** too.

Problematic Prepositions

Use prepositions to indicate the relationship between nouns, pronouns and verbs.

- The preposition **in** is used to refer to an amount of time or to an enclosed space:
  I start work **in** one week.
  Jennifer is **in** the office being interviewed now.

- The preposition **on** is used to refer to a surface or an area that is not enclosed:
  There is a booklet about summer jobs **on** the shelf.

- The preposition on is also used to refer to time:
  Heather starts her job on the first Monday of the month.

- The preposition **at** is used to refer to a location or a specific time:
  My father is **at** his new job now.
  He starts work at 9:00 a.m.

- The preposition for is used to make reference to a duration of time:
  I waited for my job training to start for one hour.

FUNCTIONAL LANGUAGE

Saying Hello and Goodbye

Nice to see you again.
What's new?
How have you been?
How are you doing?

I'd like you to meet ...
Let me introduce you to ...
Hi, my name is ...

Well, we have to get going.
See you later.

Thanks, you too.
Not much.
Great, and you?
When did you arrive?

Nice to meet you.
It's a pleasure to meet you.
Who is with ...?

OK, bye.
Yeah, take care.

Telephone Talk and Voice Mail

Hi, I'm calling about ...
May I ask who's calling?
Would you like to leave a message?
Could you ask him/her to call me back, please?

Conversation Essentials

First of all ...
However ...
On the other hand ...
Furthermore ...

Sorry to jump in ...
I hate to interrupt ...
I'd just like to add ...

All right.
I mean ...
You know ...

Just wait a second please.
Could you hold on a minute?

Making it Clear
(Requests for / offers of clarification)

What did you say?
What do you mean?
Could you repeat that, please?

What I want to say is...
What I mean is...
In other words...

Requests for Help and Information

How do you say …?
Could you give me a hand?

What does … mean?
How would you do this?

Can you tell me where …?
What will I need?
What do you think of …
When does this have to be finished?
What are we supposed to do?

Why didn't you …
Where are …?
Who knows …?

Offering Help and Feedback

Do you want me to help you with that?
I thought of something that might help.
Don't hesitate to ask for help.

If I were you, I would
What if you tried …?
What would you suggest?
He/she needs to …

I think he/she could …
He/she should try …
Why don't you …?
Could you give me your feedback on this?

Expressing Your Point of View and Making a Decision

What do you think?
How do you feel about …?
Do we all agree?
Have you come to a decision?
What would you decide?
What's your opinion?
Why not?
The best decision is …
What do you think of …?

In my opinion …
I don't think so.
I'm not sure.
It's a difficult decision.
We all agree that …
We don't agree on …
I would decide to …
I totally disagree.
I agree with …

We are having a hard time making up our minds.
Our team has a different point of view.

Feelings, Interests, Tastes and Preferences

Which would you prefer?
I feel … when …
I can't stand …
Would you like …
Given the choice, I'd …
I don't mind …
They would rather …
Which … do you want to try for?

I would rather …
I really need …
I enjoy …
I would prefer to …
Wouldn't you rather …
I would like to …
Do you enjoy …

Permission

Would you mind if I …?
Could we …?
Is it alright if …?

Capabilities

I know how to …
We might be able to …
I am sure we are capable of …
Do you think they know how to …?

Apologies

I'm sorry.
I didn't mean to …
I regret …
Please forgive me …
How can I make up for …

Warnings

Be careful.
You'd better not …
I wouldn't do that if I were you.

Suggestions and Invitations

Would you be interested in …?
Would you like to …?
What do you say we …?
Let's …

Reflecting

I was able to understand this text because …
I used this strategy to …
I did … well, but
next time I need
to focus on …

Goal Setting

I will … to improve …
Our team's goal is …
By the end of the year, I will be able to …

Teamwork and Encouragement

Let's divide the work.
Would you like to …?
Who wants to take notes?
Whose turn is it to …?
We really worked well together on that.

That's a good point.
That's a great idea.
What a great job!

STRATEGIES

Communication Strategies

Use these strategies to help you maintain a conversation:

- **Use gestures** to support your message.
- **Repeat** what someone has said to make sure that you understand.
- **Rephrase** to say it in a different way.
- **Stall for time** using functional language.
- **Substitute** with more general words or expressions when you can't be precise.

Yes. As you can see here, the colours attract the attention of younger children.

Wait a minute. I'm not sure I really understand. Do you mean that this brochure is intended for young kids?

Learning Strategies

A. Use some of the following strategies when you have a task to do.

- **Focus your attention** on particular details.
- **Pay attention** to the task at hand and ignore distractions.

I really need to listen to the language people use to give their opinion.

Come on, Vince, let's stay focused. We're almost finished.

- **Create** opportunities to practise.
- **Plan** what you will need to accomplish your task.
- **Reflect** on what you learned and how you learned it.
- **Monitor** the language you use and correct yourself when you can.
- **Set goals** and objectives for improving your English.

Learning Strategies

B. Use some of the following strategies when you are working with texts:

- **Show what you know** about the subject.
- **Predict** what the text is about by using all the cues available.
- **Skim** the text quickly to get a general overview of the text.
- **Scan** the text to find specific information.
- **Compare** similarities and differences in texts.
- **Infer** meaning by different cues in the text.
- **Take notes** as you read, listen or view texts.
- **Organize information** into more manageable blocks.
- **Recombine** the information you gather to clarify meaning.
- **Transfer** what you learn to different contexts.
- **Practise** by using what you learn in real-life situations.
- **Delay speaking** until you feel ready.

Learning Strategies

C. We learn better when we are relaxed and we feel comfortable. Some of these strategies will help you:

- **Ask for help** and clarification when necessary.
- **Ask questions**.
- **Co-operate** with others.
- **Encourage yourself** and others.
- **Develop cultural understanding** by practising often with an English speaker.
- **Stay calm**. You have all the tools you need.
- **Take risks**.
- **Congratulate yourself** on your successes.

Prcesses

The Response Process

There are three kinds of text:

Texts you **read**

Texts you **listen to**

Texts you **view**

Using some or all of the phases of the response process below can help you come to a clearer understanding of all three kinds of text.

① Explore the text

First, work on your own to come to an initial understanding of the text. Then, share your thoughts and ideas with others.

Before you read, listen or view you might :
- Use what you already know about the subject to give you ideas about the content of the text.
- Predict what the text is about by using cues such as titles, illustrations or sound effects.
- Skim the text to get a general overview.
- Select other strategies like inferencing or scanning which will help you understand the text.

While you read, listen or view you might :
- Confirm or reject the predictions you made.
- Ask yourself questions about the content.
- Organize the information.
- Identify what you think is important in the text.
- Stop and go back to a section you found difficult.

- Look up key words in the glossary boxes, vocabulary lists or a dictionary. Or ask for clarification from someone else.

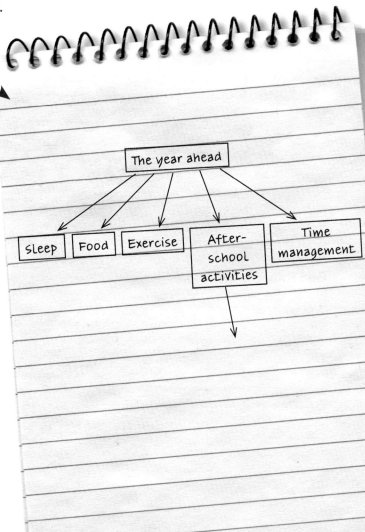

After you read, listen or view you might :
- Write down your reactions to the text in your reading log.
- Use examples from the text to support your ideas.
- Find answers to any questions you had.
- Listen to what others think about the text and modify your understanding if necessary.

I think that pirates had crazy lives.

Yes that's true, but they had a code of conduct so they were also very disciplined.

❷ **Connect with the text.**
Connect the text to your own experiences or the experiences of someone you know. Then share with others.

- Decide what was interesting or surprising in the text.
- Connect this information to your own life.
  Did the same thing ever happen to you?
  How did you react?
  How does this change your opinion of the issues in the text?
- Share your opinions with your partner.
- Use strategies and resources to compare, recombine and organize new information.

❸ **Generalize beyond the text.**
Now relate the text to your community and life in general.
- With your partner, compare situations from the text with your own reality.
- Say what is the same or different in your life.
- Decide what you could do to make people more aware of the issues.
- Refer to the text and your reading log to support your ideas.

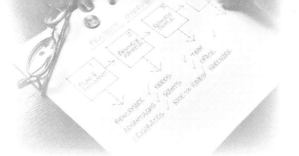

The Writing Process

Before writing, it is important to look at texts similar to the one you intend to write. This will give you ideas as to the essential components of your text. Using a writing process will help you write texts that are organized and coherent. There are five phases to the process between which you can move back and forth.

Prepare to write

Before you begin to write, set clear goals for your text.

- Brainstorm topics and ideas
- Think about what you already know concerning the subject
- Use graphs, semantic mapping or an outline to organize your ideas
- Decide on the purpose of your text
- Decide on the language you will use in your text
- Think about who your audience is
- Reflect on the topic and on the ideas you have written

Write a draft

As you write your rough copy, think about your text as a whole.

- Adjust your notes, including new ideas, as you write
- Leave space to make changes
- Reflect on what you have written
- Talk with others about what you have written

Revise

Reread your text to make sure the message is clear and the text is well organized.

- Reflect on what you have written
- Check how well you have organized your text and whether you chose the right words
- Accept and integrate feedback from your peers
- Add, substitute, delete and rearrange ideas and words

Edit

Reread your text, focusing on the grammar of your text.

- Check your sentence structure
- Verify your verbs, spelling and punctuation
- Use resources such as dictionaries and grammar references
- Use your writing checklist
- Discuss your text with your peers and the teacher
- Correct any errors
- Write a final copy

Publish

If you decide to publish your text, make sure you have a polished copy and remember to share it with your intended audience.